The Great Australian Barbecue

A BAY BOOKS PUBLICATION
An imprint of HarperCollinsPublishers

Published in Australia in 1990 by Bay Books
This edition 1992

Bay Books, of
CollinsAngus&Robertson Publishers Pty Limited
A division of HarperCollinsPublishers (Australia) Pty Limited
25 Ryde Road, Pymble NSW 2073, Australia

HarperCollinsPublishers (New Zealand) Limited
31 View Road, Glenfield, Auckland 10, New Zealand

HarperCollinsPublishers Limited
77– 85 Fulham Palace Road, London W6 8JB, United Kingdom

Barbecue ideas and techniques © Digby Brignell
Barbecue ideas and techniques © Bay Books
Barbecue and sauce recipes (72); Hints (23)
© Digby Bignell; other recipes Bay Books

National Library of Australia
Card number and ISBN 186256 315 2

Food perparation: Digby
Food Photography: Norman Nicholls
Front Cover and Barbecues: Ashley Barber
Stylist: Kay Francis
Additional Photographs:
Austral International (p. 11)
Australian Picture Library (pp 4, 7)
Weldon Trannies (pp 34, 36, 50, 67)
Printed in Australia by Griffin Press, Adelaide
5 4 3 2
95 94 93 92

The Publisher would like to thank the following
for their assistance during the photography of
this book: Craig & Seeley, Companion, Cook-
On, General Electric, Barbeques Galore, Weber,
Covered Barbeques of Australia, Dalsonware,
Rinnai (for barbecues); Crown Corning, Lifestyle
Imports, Vasa Agencies (for tableware); Orrefors
(for wooden platters); Villa Italiana (hand painted
plates); Catering Aids Pty Ltd (for stainless steel
salvers); Elof Hansson (for cutlery); Barbara's
House & Garden; Phillip & House Group
(for beach umbrella); Deeko, Hygienic-Lily,
Marimekko (for serviettes, paper plates and
cups); United Distillers (for wine and spiritts);
Weber of Adelaide (for torches); Market Imports
(for paper lanterns) and Peter's Gifts of
Kensington (for special props).

The Great Australian Barbecue

BayBooks

An imprint of HarperCollins*Publishers*

Contents

INTRODUCTION

Have you ever noticed that when people come to your home they all gather in the kitchen? Why this is, I don't know. I often wonder. It may be a throwback to days gone by when cave dwellers or members of the tribe gathered around the open fire to cook and eat. Such occasions no doubt were the beginnings of social gatherings.

What I do know is that people are generous and really like to help ('Anything I can do?'). I find this a nice human practice and trust it never stops. Now let us take this wonderful practice one step further by taking the kitchen outdoors to have a barbecue.

The barbecue is the ideal arrangement for communal cooking and generally getting together with family and friends. With our wonderful climate we can enjoy barbecuing all year round at home and on picnics.

There are a multitude of dishes that can be cooked on the barbecue ranging from seafood to meats and vegetarian. In fact, I really don't know of anything that can't be barbecued (and believe me, I have had some challenges). These dishes may be prepared and served in various ways such as individual servings on plates, or the way I prefer, as smaller portions presented on platters where your friends can either help themselves or be served by you on fresh paper napkins.

Just remember, the marvellous thing about barbecues is that you, your family and friends really have an opportunity to mingle. With this in mind, continue to experiment and you will find that the time you spend 'slaving over the hot fire' is even more enjoyable.

In the following pages you will find many helpful suggestions for cooking, eating and entertaining outdoors to add to your own ideas about this wonderful way of life. I hope my experience will help you have even better barbecues.

THE BARBECUE

To barbecue simply means to cook on an open fire. Over the centuries, since fire was discovered, people have built some sort of fireplace to cook food — especially meat or fish.

There is still nothing quite like the smell of food cooking on a barbecue and today, barbecues are more popular than ever. The only problem may be in choosing which kind best suits your needs.

Which Barbecue?

Barbecues come in many types and sizes ranging from the most basic firebowls to those with the latest features. Work out exactly what you want your barbecue for, set yourself a price limit and the rest should be plain sailing.

Your Needs

What do you plan to use your barbecue for? Obviously it is not worth investing in the top-of-the-range trolley barbecue if you eat outdoors only a couple of times a year. On the other hand, if you entertain frequently, it is equally poor value to buy a barbecue that's too small or flimsy and won't last the distance.

Portable or fixed? A permanent barbecue is great if you entertain often or eat outdoors regularly; but it needs to be positioned for summer shade and winter sun. A portable barbecue — such as the smaller rectangular or bowl-shaped one — has the advantage that you can use it both for picnics and in your garden. You can also move it around to take advantage of the sun.

Type

Grills, hotplate or covered? If you simply want to barbecue on the grill then there's the widest range of barbecues available, from the basic hibachi to a top-of-the-range trolley with all the features you can imagine. A hotplate can be useful for onions or eggs and many models combine both cooking surfaces. If you plan to entertain adventurously then you may want a rotisserie for spit-roasting. The increasingly popular covered barbecues, which can be used with the lid up for barbecuing, or closed for roasting and even smoking, certainly let you cook in the great outdoors in all weathers.

Size

Make sure that the cooking area is large enough for your needs. It is better to buy a little bigger than too small as it is important to be able to serve everyone together when eating 'al fresco'. Trolley barbecues are increasingly popular because they come in a range of sizes and most provide some preparation space as well.

Fuel

Wood Traditionally used for cooking in the great outdoors, wood is not the best fuel for barbecuing because it burns with a flame. Barbecue cooking needs heat — not flames. It is essential to let flames die down leaving a bed of red hot embers before cooking. All too often people light the fire and start barbecuing. We all know the rather charred results.

Charcoal Charcoal is essentially wood which has already been burnt down. This greatly speeds up the process of turning it into a glowing bed of heat. It is the most effective fuel for barbecuing because:
☐ it provides plenty of heat,
☐ it is ready for cooking over in 15–20 minutes,
☐ there's no smell,
☐ it can be bought in bags from department and hardware stores, and,
☐ fatty flare-ups are not a problem because you can damp to control the temperature.

A wide range of portable gas and charcoal barbecues is available. (Top, left to right) Rinnai Char Grill, Chef Gas Grill, Namco Challenger; (centre) Weber Barbecue, Waltzing Matilda; (bottom) Hibachi and Weber Table Top with hotplate

Barbecue Fuel Barbecue fuels such as Willows Heat Beads are popular for barbecuing because they can be bought in convenient sized bags and provide good heat for relatively long periods of time. Like charcoal, they have less tendency to flare up than wood. However, they are harder to light and you can't use the damping technique as successfully. They take about 30–40 minutes to reach the cooking stage. Because heat beads burn away to a very fine ash, place them on a steel sheet or a fine grate — otherwise you'll find they tend to fall through.

Gas Gas barbecues tend to be the more expensive but their big attraction is obviously their convenience: you can start barbecuing almost immediately. With the introduction of volcanic rock, gas barbecues have become even more popular. The rock is spread out below the cooking surface, absorbs the heat from the burners and glows just like charcoal or heat beads. This not only spreads the heat over a larger area but gives food an authentic barbecue favour. Gas barbecues just couldn't be easier to operate: you simply connect the gas bottle and turn on. It is always a good idea to keep a spare bottle in case the gas runs out. However, you can't use the damping technique to 'moisturise' food while cooking unless the burners are protected by a metal shield.

Electricity Electric barbecues are great for people living in apartment buildings. But they do have more limited applications because of the necessary power points and leads. Electric barbecues can also be combined with volcanic rock for that more authentic flavour.

Other Features to Consider

Stability It is essential to buy a barbecue that stands fairly and squarely on the ground. The top-of-the-range trolleys provide the maximum stability in portables. But they are also the most expensive. Smaller portables or portables with detachable or fold-away legs tend to be less stable. Check the angle of the legs and overall stability before you buy. Table models need to be looked at with the same care, although most have very short legs or supports, and are quite stable.

Cooking height Many barbecues have the cooking surface too close to the coals — we recommend that it should be at least 25–40 cm above the source of the heat. A barbecue with an adjustable height cooking surface is probably a good buy. Check also the actual height for cooking.

Materials If your barbecue lives outdoors, make sure it is made of materials that won't rust away too readily. Alternatively, invest in a cover or put that portable barbecue in the garden shed.

Shelves From the can of beer to food and sauces, you need plenty of space for putting things when barbecuing. Extra space never goes amiss, but a table alongside will do the trick. Warming racks above the barbecue are also useful, but not essential.

This trolley style barbecue has space for preparation, serving and storage. When buying a barbecue consider this and the other features mentioned above

Barbecue Cooking Techniques

There are a variety of ways to cook a barbecue, from grilling, the most popular technique, through to spit-roasting. Try wrapping vegetables in foil and putting them in the hot embers to cook, or cooking shellfish in their shells — it's delicious! Different techniques suit different cooks, and they're all listed here.

Barbecuing Barbecue grilling — cooking food on a grill over the heat — remains the most popular technique. Most of us have fond memories of succulent pieces of steak on the barbecue grill. The basic principles are to cook with heat, not flames, and retain the natural juices inside the food. Turning constantly allows the juices that run under heat to baste the food naturally. Any juices and fat which do drip, fall on the fire, vaporise and are absorbed back in the meat, adding a flavour which is unique to food barbecued this way.

It doesn't take long to barbecue foods that are up to 5 cm thick and lie flat on the barbecue, or which can be cooked in wire barbecue baskets. Larger pieces of meat can be barbecued on the grill but need to be turned constantly and watched carefully so that the outside does not burn during the longer cooking time required.

The damping technique plus constant turning ensures that food is juicy when cooked. Don't overcook. Remember that your meat, fish or poultry will continue cooking in its own heat when taken off the barbecue. So remove just before it's ready.

Damping

Damping is the key to successful barbecuing. It is such an important part of the process that you should read this paragraph twice. Damp the fire with water either from a very fine spray on your hose or by carefully sprinkling or squirting about a cup of water over the coals. This not only decreases the temperature immediately but it puts moisture back into the food with rising steam. If your barbecue grill is rather close to the coals you may wish to move the food aside as you spray or sprinkle.

Do not damp down a gas barbecue unless there is a steel shield covering the burners.

Hotplate With hotplate cooking it is the heat of the plate that cooks food rather than the direct heat of the fire. A thick plate will take longer to heat up, but will hold the heat longer than a thin one. It will also be less affected by the changes in the fire underneath, but consequently less responsive.

Essentially, using a hotplate means that you are frying your food. It is most important to have good drainage for the fat and not underestimate how much there will be. Good drainage eliminates the risk of fat running on the fire, or building up and virtually deep-frying the food. If you want to fry onions or eggs on your barbecue a frypan will do the job just as well.

The various barbecue cooking techniques: grilling, skewers and foil

Foil Vegetables in foil are popular — particularly potatoes and corn. Use heavy-duty foil or two layers and wrap food with the dull side of the foil on the outside. The parcels are placed on the grill and turned while cooking. Potatoes are great when wrapped in foil and placed in the embers.

Skewers Everything from meat, poultry, fish, fruit or vegetables can be cooked kebab style on skewers. The trick is to cut meat into same-sized pieces. Remember, with beef or lamb kebabs, cook them later for those who like them rare. The type of skewers you use is important: choose flat ones with a diamond-shaped end so that the food will stay on the skewer and will not roll around when turned. Kebab turners come battery operated so you don't have to do a thing. when cooking. Alternatively, there are kebab holders which support the skewers and you turn as required by hand.

Rotisserie Rotisserie cooking, or spit-roasting, is a challenging, but visually entertaining way to barbecue food. It also takes a long time. A whole bird, for example, is threaded on a metal spit which is then turned slowly over the fire. Rotisseries can be simple hand-turned varieties or modern battery-operated units which are much more convenient. Apart from turning, little attention is needed during cooking, though you may like to brush with a baste from about halfway through cooking time. Spit-roasting a 1.5 kg chicken would take 1½ hours.

To speed up cooking time and ensure even cooking, fit reflectors to the sides of the barbecue at the height of the food. They may detract from the visual impact of spit-roasting, but the benefits outweigh this by far. To prevent flare-ups, place a drip tray directly under the meat to catch the fat.

Covered barbecues Barbecues with a lid are more like an outdoor oven enabling you to bake, grill and smoke food. You adjust the dampers to increase or reduce the temperature or maintain the required heat.

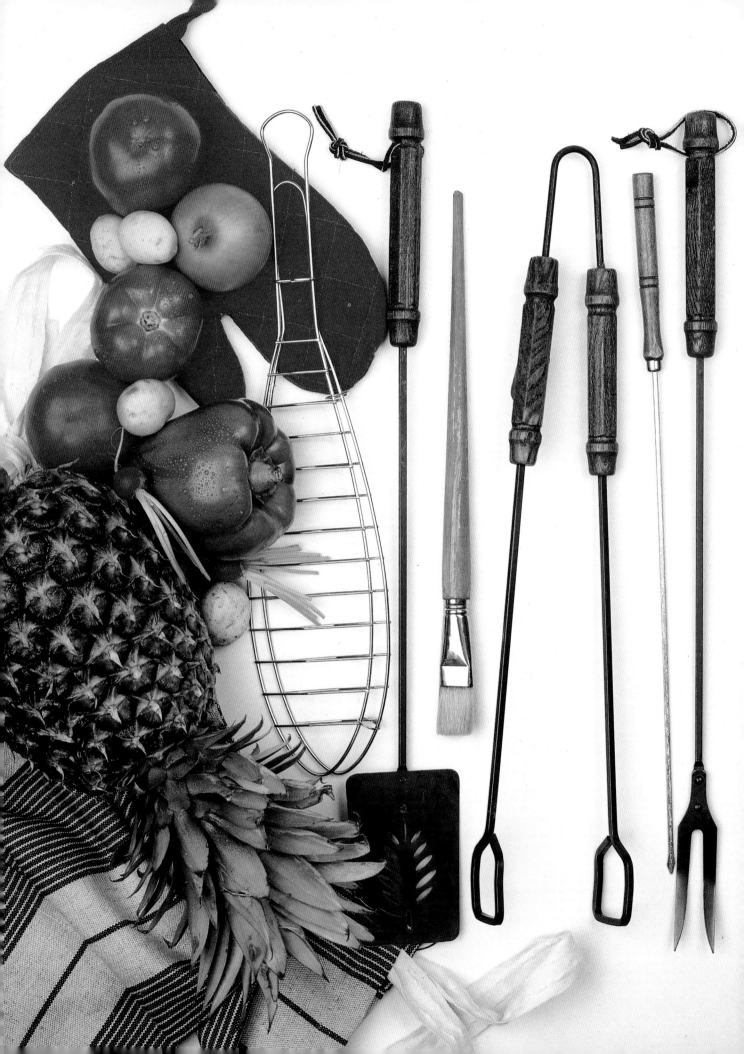

The Basic Essentials of Barbecue Equipment

Like the range of barbecues available, the accessories and equipment you buy really depend on your needs. There's no need to rush out and buy everything. Take a long hard look in your kitchen cupboards first. There are usually tongs or pots and pans which can be retired to start a new life as barbecue equipment. Keep all your barbecue equipment together — then you always have it when you need it.

Ensure that all equipment is sturdy and will stand up to rough treatment. All handles should be insulated and long enough to keep the cook's hands clear of the cooking surface. A list of basics should include:

Long-handled tongs — for adjusting hot coals and turning food

Long-handled fork — for turning food or pricking sausages

Long-handled spatula — for turning foods that tend to fall apart such as hamburgers and fish

Stiff metal brush — for scrubbing the grill

Butcher's knife — for trimming meat

Parer knife — for fruit and vegetables

Basting brush — for dabbing bastes and sauces over food. Small 5 cm wide paint brushes are suitable

Skewers — for kebabs. Flat, metal skewers with an insulated handle are best. If using bamboo satay sticks, soak them in water beforehand.

Barbecue wire baskets — for holding large pieces of food like whole fish. You can buy these or make them yourself using galvanised steel mesh

Heavy duty aluminum foil — for wrapping potatoes, vegetables or bread

Frypan — a long-handled cast iron pan can be used in place of a hotplate for cooking onions, eggs and spectacular flambes

Pots — small saucepans are useful for heating sauces on the side of the barbecue

Crockery and cutlery — sturdy, non-breakable varieties are best and bright colours brighten the party atmosphere

Oven mitt or cloth — essential to prevent burnt fingers. Make sure mitts are comfortable

Apron — sturdy is best to guard against splatters

Aerosol vegetable oil spray — for greasing

Hairpin skewers

Make yourself some hairpin style skewers for cooking kebabs. Bend stainless steel wire into hairpin-shaped skewers about 20 cm long and 1.5 cm wide (you can make them while you watch television).

Basic barbecue equipment includes (clockwise from top): an oven mitt, wire basket, long-handled spatula, a brush, tongs, skewers, long-handled fork and apron

Extra Accessories

There is an enormous range of attachments, accessories and gadgets designed for the modern barbecue. Few are essential, but many prove very handy for specialised cooking, particularly if you like entertaining. They are often expensive, so make sure you will be able to make good use of them.

Rotisseries Rotisseries can be simple hand-operated types or more expensive battery-charged models. When buying, make sure it fits your particular barbecue. Look for a sturdy spit that will not bend and a heavy-duty motor that will keep on turning.

Kebab turner The simplest kind is just a metal box with a series of notches cut into the top of each long side to hold the skewers. Alternatively, you can purchase a motorised version which automatically turns the skewers as well.

Meat thermometer This long probe with a temperature dial at one end is inserted into the meat or poultry before cooking. As the meat cooks, the dial indicates the internal temperature. A meat thermometer ensures there are no nasty surprises when serving. Often it is easy to assume the meat is ready because of the external appearance, when in fact it is still uncooked inside. The thermometer eliminates error. Meat thermometers are particularly useful for spit roasting and when using a covered barbecue. They are absolutely essential if you are barbecuing a whole pig or lamb.

Wok holders The development of the barbecue wok holder has brought the delights and diversity of Asian foods to outdoor eating, greatly increasing the cook's repertoire. Make sure you use the right shaped wok — one with a curved base.

Gas lighters These are essential for owners of gas barbecues. It is often impractical to light gas burners with matches.

Electric starters These are used for lighting charcoal.

A fire extinguisher or fire blanket Either of these would be a sensible purchase. Both will quickly extinguish a fire in an emergency.

Trout in wire baskets

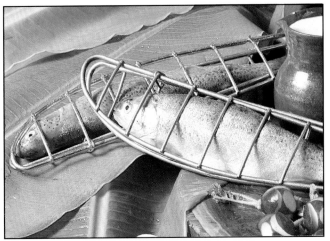

A tasty marinade adds flavour to pork

Using Marinades and Bastes

Good quality meat, fish or poultry does not need marinating before it is cooked. Marinades tenderise the cheaper cuts of meat. Most marinades usually contain an acid (such as vinegar, lemon juice or wine) to tenderise the fibres; an oil to moisturise; and herbs, spices or seasonings for flavour.

Marinating, however, contributes spicy flavours to the barbecue banquet. Dabbing with a baste or prepared sauce just before the end of cooking time is all that's required with good quality meats. You simply apply the sauce like a light glaze.

Flare-ups

Flare-ups can be a minor problem when barbecuing. They are caused by fat dripping on the fire. The best way to prevent these is to trim virtually all the visible fat off the meat first and to set your grill 25–40 cm above the coals. Control flare-ups by the damping technique or, on gas barbecues, by moving the food to one side or turning down the heat. Flames simply burn food on the outside and leave the inside raw.

14

1. Place firestarters among charcoal on base of barbecue

2. Arrange more charcoal over burning firestarters

Lighting the Barbecue

Lighting the fire properly is integral to the success of a barbecue meal. Charcoal and heat beads require firestarters, while 'deal' and twigs will do for wood. If air is able to circulate, the fire will get going faster. If you are cooking more than one dish, start with a course like sausages, as the fatty drips will drive the fire on faster.

Wood   Collect plenty of wood in varying sizes. Light the fire with paper, dry twigs and leaves. Add larger pieces of wood carefully when the fire is established.

Charcoal   Charcoal lights readily with firestarters. Arrange a layer of charcoal about 5 cm deep on the barbecue, placing firestarters strategically on the base at about 15 cm intervals. When they are alight, place more charcoal carefully on top, then let them burn out. This takes about 10–15 minutes and by now the charcoal is ready for you to begin cooking.

Heat beads   These can be a little more difficult to light. Once again you need firestarters. Arrange the beads in a pile with the starters. A grey ash will appear when the beads are alight. If they don't catch, begin the whole process again. Never pour a flammable liquid over heat beads to get them going.

Ready for Cooking?

Whatever your fuel, you need to know when to start cooking the food on the barbecue grill. With wood, the fires should have burnt down to red hot embers. With charcoal and heat beads, wait until the fuel is partially covered by a grey ash. Judge an electrical or gas-heated grill the same as you would in your kitchen. Some foods need to be cooked quickly over a good hot fire. Others take more time over a low heat.

Good hot   This is the hottest fire. If you place your hand near the grill, the heat will be intolerable after just two or three seconds.

Medium hot   This versatile temperature is suitable for most barbecued foods. Your hand near the grill could tolerate this heat for three or four seconds.

Low heat   You should be able to keep your hand near the grill for four or five seconds. This heat is for thicker foods which need cooking for a longer period of time.

Temperature Control

Constant monitoring and control of temperatures is just as important for barbecuing as it is for gourmet cooking. Gas and electric barbecues can be easily turned up or down. You have just as much control with a charcoal barbecue fuel fire because you simply damp it down when it gets too hot. Throughout cooking, top up fire with more charcoal every 15–20 minutes. On kettle-style barbecues, adjusting the air vents gives you good control over the fire.

SEAFOOD

Whole fish, shellfish and even fish fillets and steaks can be cooked on the barbecue. The secret of success is to make sure that you don't overcook your fish. It is ready when it is just flaky. Control the heat by damping during cooking. Damping creates steam which replaces any moisture lost in cooking. On a gas barbecue, where you can't damp, move food to the cooler areas on the sides, or turn down the burners.

Prepare your seafood in the usual way and make up the sauces you will need in advance. They can sit warming in a pot at the side of the barbecue while you work.

Wire barbecue baskets are ideal for cooking whole fish. There's nothing nicer than seeing a whole fish cooking on the fire. Grease baskets lightly in advance with a vegetable oil or spray. Then simply clamp the prepared fish in the basket and cook turning frequently. Score large fish two or three times for even heat penetration. You can insert lemon juice or spices in the cuts for added flavour. Because fish can be delicate to handle, some people prefer to cook them in foil. If you do, choose a heavy-duty foil or use two layers to prevent tearing.

How much fish? Quantities depend on how many people you are serving and how big their appetites are. Base amounts on what you usually serve, remembering that people often eat more in the open air. Allow about 250 g whole fish and about 4–6 king prawns per person. Buy prawns or smaller fish like trout graded the same size, so that your guests can all be served their hot food at the same time.

The essence of barbecuing any food is creativity and imagination. These seafood recipes are all designed with that flexibility in mind.

Also, there are many savoury butters and sauces suitable for the seafood barbecue (see *Sauces, Bastes and Butters* recipes).

All seafood: Simple Seafood Butter Sauce; Basil or Dill Butters.

Grilled Fish: Parsley Lemon Butter; Caper, Spiked Seafood, Sweet and Sour Sauces.

Shellfish: Bercy Butter; Easy Garlic, Avocado, Curry or Sate Sauces.

Kebabs

Kebabs — meat, chicken and seafood — are popular, but turning skewers can be tricky. Whether turning by hand or using a special battery operated kebab turner, make sure to use skewers that will hold food firmly. With round skewers, food rolls around too when you try to turn. With flat skewers or notched skewers, your meat, chicken or fish stays in place.

Seafood Kebabs

small to medium-sized
uncooked prawns
large scallops with the roe
attached

Shell and devein prawns and remove tails. Thread scallops and prawns alternately on lightly greased skewers and barbecue over a good hot fire, turning occasionally. When nearly cooked, dab kebabs with a seafood sauce (*see recipes*). Barbecue time about 10 minutes.

Spicy Kebabs

1 kg ling or barramundi
fillets
melted butter

Marinade
2 cloves garlic, crushed
2 onions, very finely
chopped
⅔ cup natural yoghurt
salt
½ teaspoon ground ginger
½ teaspoon chilli powder
2 teaspoons garam masala

Wash and dry fish and cut into cubes. Combine marinade ingredients, pour over fish and leave in refrigerator for 2 hours.

Thread fish onto 12 skewers and grill over a hot fire, 3–4 minutes each side. Baste fish with melted butter while cooking. Serve hot. Barbecue time about 10 minutes.

Serves 4–6

Spicy Kebabs

Whole fish to be prepared for barbecueing. Fish can be basted with a tasty marinade while cooking

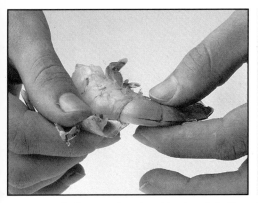

1. Remove head and legs and shell prawn

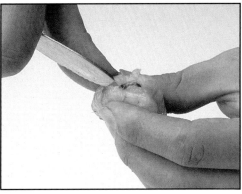

2. To devein, nick vein section at top

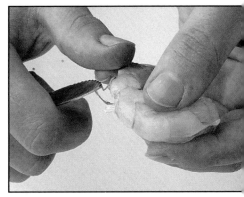

3. Make a small cut to expose vein just above tail. Pull vein through

King Prawn Kebabs with (from left) Curry, Easy Garlic and Sate Sauces

---

In the basket

A wire basket lets you handle large foods which have to be turned. Whole fish can simply be clamped into the basket — not too tight — and turned as required to cook evenly right through. Prepare baskets by lightly greasing with oil or spraying with a non-stick spray coating.

King Prawn Kebabs

uncooked king prawns or
kingprawn cutlets with
tails on, graded same size

Shell and devein prawns leaving the tail on. Thread prawns on skewers (about 4 prawns per skewer) and barbecue over a good hot fire turning frequently. The cooking time will depend on the size of prawns you use. When they are just about ready, brush prawns with your own specialty sauce or any of the following suggestions: Chilli, Curry, Easy Garlic and Sate or Simple Seafood Butter Sauces (*see recipes*). Arrange prawns on platter and serve. Barbecue time about 10–15 minutes.

Fish Kebabs

750 g firm fish fillets

Marinade
½ cup oil
½ cup lemon juice
½ cup dry white wine
salt and pepper
dried rosemary or basil

Cut fish fillets into pieces 5 cm square. Combine marinade ingredients, pour over fish pieces and leave for at least 2 hours in refrigerator.

Thread fish pieces on lightly greased skewers, allowing about 6 pieces per person, and cook over a medium fire, turning and basting occasionally with remaining marinade. Barbecue time about 5 minutes.

Serves 4

Scallops and Lychees in Bacon

rindless bacon rashers
fresh scallops with the roe
  attached
canned lychees
lemon juice
freshly ground black pepper

Cut bacon into 7.5 cm lengths and lychees in half. On each strip of bacon, place half a lychee and a whole scallop. Roll up and thread on small skewers. Allow about 2 rolls per skewer. Barbecue over a good hot fire turning occasionally and taking care that the flame does not touch the food. Serve with lemon juice and pepper. Barbecue time about 10 minutes.

Alternative Fruits: Dried apricots, dried apples or dried dates cut into halves (fresh dates are too soft).

Flambe Scallops

100 g butter, melted or a
  good splash of oil
500 g fresh scallops with the
  roe attached
150 mL gin or vodka
2 avocados, halved and
  seeded

Melt butter in a pan over a good hot fire taking care not to let it burn. Add scallops, gently tossing for 5 minutes. When cooked, quickly pour over warmed gin and ignite. Toss scallops until flame dies away then serve piled on fresh avocado halves. Barbecue time about 5 minutes.

Serves 4

Flambe Scallops

Scallops and Lychees in Bacon served with salad

Whisky Prawns

16 uncooked king prawns
  (4 per person)
100 g butter
1–2 tablespoons lemon
  juice
150 mL whisky, warmed or
  Grand Marnier, warmed
4–6 large lettuce leaves,
  washed and dried

Shell and devein prawns removing the tails. Over a good hot fire, melt butter in cast iron pan or wok, add lemon juice and prawns and toss taking care not to burn the butter. When prawns are almost cooked, remove from fire, pour over warmed whisky and ignite. Keep tossing prawns until the flame dies away. Serve immediately on a bed of fresh lettuce leaves. Barbecue time about 5–10 minutes.

Serves 4

Flambe — delicious and spectacular

Use an attractive solid cast iron or aluminum pan, or a wok on a stand for flambe dishes. (Make sure the wok has a curved, not flat base.) Place on your barbecue over a good hot fire, cook your food, warm the alcohol, remove food from fire, pour and ignite!

Crayfish Tails

uncooked same-sized
  crayfish tails
butter
salt and pepper
lemon wedges

Make a full-length, deep cut along underside of each crayfish and insert thin slices of butter. Place tails in wire barbecue basket and over a medium to hot fire, cook whole, shell down for about three-quarters of the cooking time. This means they will tend to cook in their own juice. Take care not to burn the shell by damping the charcoal to control heat. On a gas barbecue, move food to the cooler sides to control temperature or turn the burners down. When tails are nearly cooked, brush with melted butter and lemon juice.

Chop into bite-sized portions — you should get about 6–8 portions per tail — and serve with lemon wedges and salt and pepper to taste. Hollandaise Sauce (*see recipe*) goes well with crayfish. Barbecue time about 30–40 minutes.

Barbecued Crayfish

4 medium-sized crayfish
  tails, fresh or frozen
1/4 cup melted butter
2 tablespoons lemon juice
2 cloves garlic, crushed
1 tablespoon French
  mustard
1 tablespoon grated orange
  rind
1 teaspoon ground ginger

Cut off thin undershell of crayfish with kitchen scissors. Bend tail back to crack shell, or insert long skewers lengthways, between shell and meat, to prevent curling. Combine remaining ingredients and brush crayfish tails with this. Grill over hot coals for 5 minutes with meat uppermost. Turn and grill 5–10 minutes until meat loses its transparency. Top with remaining garlic butter and serve. Barbecue time about 15 minutes.

Serves 4–6

Crayfish Tails

Barbecued Abalone

fresh or frozen abalone
butter
lemon wedges
chopped fresh parsley, to
  garnish

Wash and clean abalone, making sure the gut and black mantle are removed. Cut abalone into paper thin slices and tenderise by pounding with a meat mallet.

Cook abalone slices on a medium hot plate for 1–2 minutes and serve hot with butter, lemon wedges and parsley garnish. Alternatively, serve with a seafood sauce or butter (*see Sauces, Bastes and Butters*).

Serves depend on size of abalone

Take care

Most burns from barbecuing result from absentmindedness, so keep your mind on the job. Immerse minor burns in cold water for around 10 minutes. Don't use lotions or ointments, simply cover with a sterile dry gauze and bandage. In the case of scalding, apply a bandage very lightly. In severe cases seek medical attention promptly.

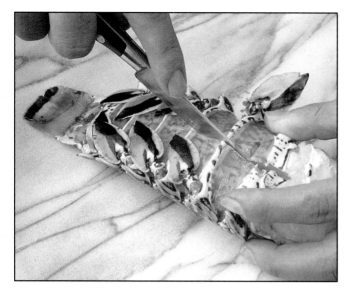

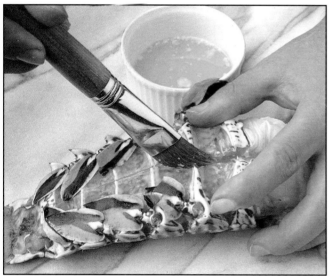

1. Make deep cut along underside of crayfish tail
2. Insert thin slices of butter or dab melted butter
3. Chop into serving pieces

Marinated Abalone

fresh or frozen abalone
  (1 per person)
low-salt soy sauce

Wash and clean abalone, making sure the gut and black mantle are removed.

Soak abalone in soy sauce for 1½–2 hours. Place whole abalone on a very low-heat part of the hotplate and cook for 2 hours, or until meat is tender.

Barbecued Mussels

mussels in shells (choose
  tightly closed shells)
Herb Butter (see recipe)

Wash and clean mussel shells. Place mussels on a medium hotplate and cook for 2–3 minutes or until shells pop open. Dab Herb Butter into the shells and cook until butter is melted.

Note: New Zealand mussels are sold with shells open. Dab Herb Butter in each mussel and cook mussels on a medium hotplate for 2–3 minutes or until all the meat has changed colour.

Alternatively cook mussels in a favourite sauce such as tomato sauce. Have a pot of fresh tomatoes, chopped onion, garlic and fresh herbs simmering on the side of the barbecue. Cook the mussels in the sauce until either the shells pop open or the mussel meat changes colour. Serve with sauce. Barbecue time 2–3 minutes.

Herbed Pipis (Eugaries)

pipis in shells (shells must
  be tightly closed)
Herb Butter (see recipe)

Soak pipis in fresh water for 2–3 hours. This removes the grit and sand from the meat.

Put the pipis on a medium hotplate and cook until shells open. Dab Herb Butter in each pipi and cook until butter melts. Barbecue time 2–3 minutes.

Whole Queensland Mud Crabs

same-sized live Queensland
  mud crabs (½–1 per
  person)
pepper
lemon wedges

Place crabs in freezer for about 30 minutes to kill. Remove, place in wire barbecue basket and cook shell down over a good hot fire. Turn three-quarters of the way through cooking time.

When cooked, allow to cool slightly then break open and cut into serving pieces. Serve with pepper, lemon wedges or Avocado Sauce (see recipe). Barbecue time about 30 minutes per kilogram.

1. Scale with a teaspoon, scraping from to tail to head under running water

2. Trim tail and fins

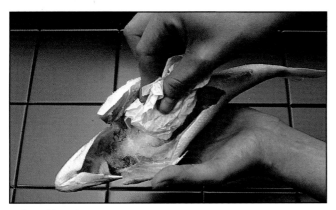

3. Sprinkle salt in cavity, wipe and rinse

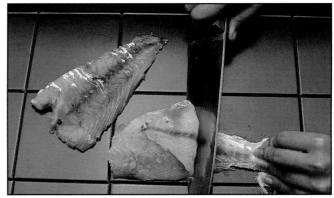

4. To skin fillets work from tail to head at a 45° angle

Preparing a Whole Fish

To prepare a whole fish for cooking, wipe it over with a damp cloth and check for scales near the head and fins. If further scaling is necessary, use a teaspoon and scrape lightly but firmly from the tail to the head on both sides. This is best done under running water because the scales then collect in the sink and can easily be discarded.

Trim fins and neaten the tail with a pair of kitchen scissors if you like. The eyes can be removed but may be better left in because when they turn white you know the fish is cooked. If you find them unsightly, cover them with a garnish before serving.

Open the cavity of the fish and sprinkle about 2 teaspoons of salt into it. Take a wad of kitchen paper and clean well down the backbone to remove any blood spots. Rinse well with cold water. Pat the fish dry, cover and refrigerate until used.

Chicken/seafood marinades

Try using your favourite chicken marinade on seafood. As a general rule, marinades for chicken are also ideal for seafood.

Barbecued Whole Smoked Fish

whole smoked gemfish,
  blue cod or tailor

Place whole fish in greased wire barbecue basket and clamp. Barbecue over a medium fire, skin down, for about three-quarters of the cooking time. Turn and cook other side. Serve with lemon wedges or Avocado Sauce (*see recipe*). Barbecue time about 20 minutes per kilogram.

Barbecued Trout

same-sized whole trout
  (1 per person)

Prepare wire barbecue baskets by greasing with vegetable oil or spraying. Clean trout and pat dry. Place in basket and barbecue over a medium fire turning frequently and taking care not to scorch skin during cooking. Finely sliced almonds, placed in trout cavity before cooking, provide a tasty variation.

Serve with Bearnaise or Hollandaise Sauces (*see recipes*), with slivered toasted almonds or with lemon wedges and salt and pepper to taste. Barbecue time about 15 minutes per 500 g.

Stuffed Fish

1 kg whole fish, gutted and
  scaled
salt
juice 1 lemon
30 g butter

Stuffing
2 tablespoons olive oil
1 small onion, finely
  chopped
3 tablespoons chopped
  celery leaves
2 tablespoons chopped
  fresh parsley
1 cup fresh breadcrumbs
salt and pepper
juice ½ lemon
1 egg, beaten

Sauce
1 tablespoon olive oil
1 onion, finely chopped
1 green capsicum, seeded
  and sliced
4 tomatoes, peeled and
  chopped
pinch cayenne pepper
juice ½ lemon
2 tablespoons water
2 tablespoons chopped
  fresh parsley

Clean fish, season with salt and sprinkle with lemon juice. Set aside while preparing stuffing.

In a wok heat oil and fry onion for 2 minutes. Add celery leaves and parsley and cook for a further 2 minutes. Stir through breadcrumbs and season with salt, pepper and lemon juice. Cool for a few minutes and stir in beaten egg.

Place breadcrumb stuffing in cavity of fish and secure the opening with skewers. Wrap fish in foil and dot with butter. Barbecue over a medium heat for 25–30 minutes or until fish flakes easily when tested.

While fish is barbecuing prepare sauce. Heat oil and fry onion for 2 minutes. Add green capsicum and tomatoes and cook for a further 3 minutes. Stir through cayenne, lemon juice and water. Bring to the boil, reduce heat and simmer until sauce is thick. Stir in parsley.

When the fish is cooked remove to a serving dish and pour sauce over. Serve hot with boiled rice. Barbecue time 35–40 minutes.

Serves 4

Stuffed Fish

Bream and Orange

2 large oranges, peeled and
    segmented
1 large onion, finely sliced
2 cloves garlic, crushed
40 g butter
2 tablespoons fresh
    chopped parsley
pepper
1 cup bean sprouts
½ cup slivered almonds,
    toasted
½ cup red and green
    capsicum, seeded and
    chopped
2 x 1 kg whole silver bream
1¼ cups orange juice
fresh Italian parsley, to
    garnish

Dice half the orange segments. In a wok, lightly saute onion and garlic with butter. Add diced orange segments, parsley and pepper and cook lightly a further 2 minutes. Add bean sprouts, almonds and capsicum.

Trim fish tail and fins and remove any scales still attached. Season cavity then stuff each with orange and onion mixture. Wrap fish in foil and barbecue over medium fire. Cooking time is 15 minutes per 500 g. Arrange remaining orange segments over fish and garnish with parsley. Serve hot dividing each fish into 4 equal pieces. Barbecue time is about 30 minutes.

Serves 2–4

Fish In Foil

2 x 1.5–2 kg whole cleaned
    fish (whiting, bream or
    mullet)
2 lemons
salt and pepper
3 onions, sliced in rings
250 g mushrooms, sliced
4 tomatoes, sliced
80 g butter
lemon wedges, to serve

Remove scales and wipe fish with a damp cloth. Peel rind from 1 lemon, cut into julienne strips and simmer in water for a few minutes; drain and cool. Squeeze lemons and brush lemon juice over both fish. Season with salt and pepper. Place fish on 2 large pieces of aluminum foil, shiny side down. Spread onion rings over both fish, then cover with mushrooms and tomatoes. Dot butter over fish. Drizzle over any remaining lemon juice and sprinkle with rind. Wrap fish in foil, forming a seal on one side.

Cook fish over glowing coals until done — cooking time will depend on heat of fire and thickness of fish. Serve fish with the vegetables and cooking juices. Garnish with lemon wedges. Barbecue time about 25–40 minutes.

Serves 10–12

Barbecued Whole Fish

whole fish in season such as
    bream, barramundi,
    snapper, whiting

Scale, clean and pat fish dry. Make a couple of cuts and insert lemon or spices if you like. Place fish in greased wire barbecue basket and barbecue over medium fire. Cooking time depends on size of fish. Turn basket frequently throughout cooking time. Serve with lemon wedges and salt and pepper to taste or with Mornay Sauce (see recipe). Barbecue time about 15 minutes per 500 g.

Grilled Trout

2 eggs
1 tablespoon cream
1 teaspoon chopped fresh
    parsley
1 clove garlic, crushed
½ teaspoon ground allspice
8 same-sized trout
8 rindless bacon rashers

Beat eggs with cream, parsley, garlic and allspice. Coat trout, inside and out, with this mixture. Place a bacon rasher in each trout and barbecue until fish flakes with a fork. Serve with a light seafood sauce (see recipes). Barbecue time about 15 minutes.

Serves 8

Grilled Trout

A barbecue banquet. Clockwise from top: Barbecued Whole
Fillet, Tandoori Chicken, Prawns and Sate Sauce, Fish in Foil

Bombay Fish Curry

1 kg whole snapper, gutted,
   scaled and cleaned
salt
60 g ghee
1 small onion, finely
   chopped
1 clove garlic, crushed
½ teaspoon grated fresh
   ginger
2 dried red chillies, seeded
   and finely chopped
2 teaspoons ground
   coriander
1 teaspoon turmeric
1 teaspoon ground mustard
   seed
½ teaspoon ground chillies
300 mL coconut milk
   bought or homemade
   (see recipe following)
juice 1 lime

Wipe fish inside and out. Sprinkle backbone with salt and rub in with a wad of kitchen paper. Rinse cavity well and pat dry. Heat ghee in a wok or cast iron pan large enough to hold fish. Add onion, garlic and ginger. Cook slowly until soft and golden. Add chillies and spices and cook further 2–3 minutes. Add coconut milk and bring to the boil, reduce heat, taste and adjust the seasoning with salt and lime juice. Simmer sauce until slightly thickened.

Place fish in pan, spoon over some of the sauce and cook over a gentle heat until fish is tender, about 20 minutes. Shake pan occasionally to prevent fish sticking. Serve hot with rice. Barbecue time about 30 minutes.

Serves 4

Coconut Milk

1 cup desiccated coconut
300 mL warm water

Blend coconut with warm water, until smooth. Strain through fine strainer, muslin or chux, and squeeze to extract milk.

Herbed Fish Grill

1 large whole fish
olive oil
salt and pepper
fresh fennel sprigs
1 glass brandy

Clean and dry fish. Brush with olive oil and season with salt and pepper. Lay branches of fennel across the fish on both sides and place in wire grilling basket. Grill on both sides until flesh flakes easily when tested with a fork. Sprinkle with more oil occasionally. When cooked, lay flesh on a fireproof platter, sprinkle with snipped fennel, douse with brandy and set alight. When flames die down, serve with lemon wedges and Sauce Remoulade (see recipe). Serves depend on size of fish. Barbecue time about 15–30 minutes per kilogram, depending on type of fish.

Prawns in their shells with Curry Sauce and Bombay Fish Curry

Fish Fillets and Cutlets

Fish fillets and cutlets are delicious barbecued. They can be cooked on the barbecue grill, or in foil over a medium to hot fire. If you are grilling over charcoal, damp the fire occasionally to replace lost moisture. If using gas, control heat carefully.

If cooking fish fillets in foil, combine your favourite vegetables — thinly sliced carrots, onions, tomatoes, potatoes, leeks, shallots — and fresh herbs with the fish. Wrap the fish in foil and cook on a medium hotplate for 5–10 minutes, depending on fillet thickness.

Do not overcook fish when barbecuing. When the flesh is just flaky the fish is ready to eat. Cooking time depends on thickness. Allow about 4–5 minutes a side for 2.5 cm thick fish cutlets. Turn carefully to cook other side. Carefully brush with Seafood or Bearnaise Sauce (see recipes) just before the end of cooking time and serve hot.

Marinating fish adds extra favour to seafood. Popular marinade ingredients include lemon juice, white wine, oil, finely diced shallots or onion, soy or teriyaki sauces, fresh ginger and fresh herbs to taste. Marinades can also be used for basting during cooking (see Sauces, Bastes and Butters).

Sole Fillets en Papillote

30 g butter
60 g mushrooms, thinly
   sliced
½ cup dry white wine
1 tablespoon finely
   chopped onion
1 teaspoon cornflour
2 tablespoons lemon juice
4 fillets sole
375 g shelled school prawns
1 tablespoon chopped fresh
   parsley

Melt butter and gently fry mushrooms until soft. Add wine and finely chopped onion and cook 1 minute. Blend cornflour with a little water and add to the mushroom mixture. Stir until boiling. Simmer 1 minute then pour in lemon juice.

Place sole fillets on lightly greased double layer of foil. Top with prawns, pour over sauce, sprinkle with parsley and wrap fish securely. Barbecue over medium heat until fish is tender. Barbecue time about 20 minutes.

Serves 4

Cooking fish

Avoid overcooking fish. It just becomes dried out and tasteless. Properly cooked fish is moist, tender and full of flavour. It is ready to eat when the flesh is just starting to flake.

POULTRY

Poultry has long been popular at barbecues with both cooks and guests. It's a flexible ingredient and a convenient finger food. Whole chickens can be spit-roasted in 1–1½ hours, chicken pieces basted and barbecued and fillets from the breast or thigh cut into bite-sized chunks and served as kebabs or sates. For extra spicy flavour, marinate chicken pieces first or serve with tasty dipping or pouring sauces and plenty of napkins. For those with really hearty appetites, take advantage of the specialty counters where you can buy turkey drumsticks and wings.

The key to successful poultry barbecuing lies in temperature control and timing. It is important that poultry does not undercook, overcook, or burn. Cook over a medium to hot fire damping the charcoal to control the temperature. When using gas, move food to the cooler sides or even lift off for a moment. Overcooked poultry tends to be stringy and tasteless. It's time to serve when joints move freely or the juices run clear when thigh flesh is pierced.

Whole chickens look great on the rotisserie: simply truss your bird and arrange on a spit with the drip pan below. Many of the latest barbecues have rotisserie accessories or can be fitted with rotisseries which turn automatically. To ensure even cooking and speed up cooking time, remember what the boy scouts do: fit reflectors to the sides of the barbecue to the height of the food. The reflector bounces the heat from the fire to the place where it's needed — the chicken. Fitting reflectors — metal baking tins will do — may detract from the appearance but certainly contributes to cooking.

Poultry can also be cooked in foil, but since most people like the skin golden, it should be crisped on the barbecue before serving.

Quantities depend on how many people you are planning to serve — and what else you have on the barbecue. A 1 kg size chicken will be plenty for two people and leave you something for chicken sandwiches next day. If you have an especially popular recipe, remember to allow for second helpings. Fresh air does wonders for appetites.

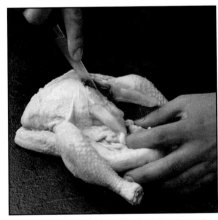

1. To portion chicken, lie it on back and cut through breast

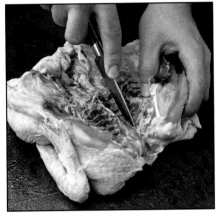

2. Expose breastbone and cut down each side

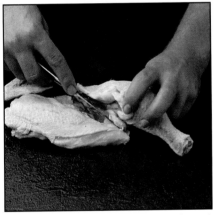

3. Separate Maryland section from breast

4. Pull back drumstick and cut to joint

5. Break open drumstick to joint and now cut right through

6. Hold wing and cut into joint to separate from breast

Barbecued Chicken pieces served with salad

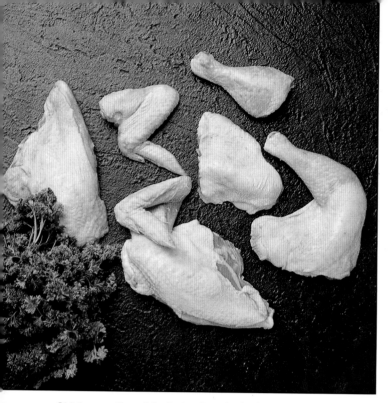

Chicken portions (clockwise from top): drumstick, thigh, Maryland section, half breast, breast and wing

Tandoori Chicken

Tandoori chicken is an Indian dish, traditionally marinated in a spicy yoghurt mixture and cooked in a special oven called a tandoor.

unflavoured yoghurt
fruit yoghurt, such as
    apricot
Tandoori Mix, bought or
    homemade (see recipe
    following)
fresh 1 kg chickens or
    chicken pieces

Prepare a yoghurt marinade by mixing together natural and fruit yoghurts and the Tandoori Mix you have made or bought. For two x 1 kg chickens you would need 1 kg natural yoghurt and 250 g fruit yoghurt. Try the taste test to make sure you have the spicy marinade mixed to suit your palate.

Cut chicken into portions, immerse in marinade for at least 1 hour prior to cooking (the longer the better). Drain and arrange pieces on barbecue grill over a medium fire. Keep wings to the outside, as they do not take as long to cook. Barbecue time about 30 minutes.

If you prefer you can barbecue half chickens this way or spit-roast whole chickens, although the cooking times will be longer. A spit-roasted chicken will take about 1–1½ hours to cook.

Tandoori Mix

1 large onion
4 cloves garlic, peeled
½ teaspoon ground ginger
½ teaspoon ground
    coriander
½ teaspoon ground cumin
chilli powder to taste (no
    more than 1/2 teaspoon)
2 teaspoons salt
1 tablespoon vinegar or
    juice 1 lemon

Grind onion and garlic together to a paste. Add seasonings, mix thoroughly then stir in lemon juice.

Always buy good quality chicken, turkey or duck and same-sized pieces so that you can serve everyone hot food at the same time.

If you want to enhance the favour of barbecued poultry there are a number of marinades and sauces you can make or buy. There's nothing wrong in taking advantage of the wonderful gourmet products on the market. Try some of the suggested sauces and bastes: Apricot or Paw Paw Baste add fruitier flavours, or try Poultry Wine Baste; Herb Butter is delicious with grilled chicken and so are sauces such as Digby's Special, Sate and Plum and Chilli (see recipes).

Barbecued Mustard Chicken

1 kg chicken pieces

Marinade
125 g butter
3 tablespoons mild mustard
1 tablespoon
    Worcestershire sauce
2 teaspoons dried rosemary
2 teaspoons chopped fresh
    parsley
1 teaspoon salt and freshly
    ground black pepper

Melt butter and add all other marinade ingredients. Dip chicken pieces into this mixture and leave for 1 hour at least. When required grill over hot coals, turning and basting with remaining marinade, until chicken is tender. Barbecue time about 15 minutes.

Serves 4–6

Billy tea

Nothing adds a more authentic Australian touch to a barbecue than boiling the billy. Place as many cups of water into the billy as you think will be consumed. When the water is boiling add one teaspoon of tea to every two cups of water and a gum leaf. Let the billy stand for five minutes, while tea leaves settle, then enjoy your cuppa! But be careful if your guests want you to spin the billy!

30

Spit-roasted Herbed Chicken

125 g butter
fresh herbs to taste,
 tarragon, oregano
1 clove garlic, crushed
3 x 1 kg chickens, trussed

Allowing a 1 kg chicken for 2 people should leave you enough for a tasty chicken salad next day. Enclose barbecue with reflectors for even cooking.

Melt butter and add herbs and crushed garlic. Barbecue chickens on rotisserie over a good hot fire brushing occasionally with butter and herb baste from halfway through cooking time. The chickens are ready when the juice runs clear if you pierce the thigh. Barbecue time about 1–1½ hours.

Serves 6

Barbecued Chicken Halves

fresh 1 kg chickens or
 chicken halves
100–150 g butter, melted
selected sauce (see recipes)

Wash and dry chickens and split in half. Arrange in greased wire basket and barbecue over a medium fire. Control heat. Place skin side down on barbecue to crisp first. After 5–10 minutes, turn over. Two-thirds of cooking time will be skin side up. Just before serving, brush with melted butter. Heat prepared sauce on side of barbecue and serve with chicken halves. Barbecue time about 30–35 minutes.

Suggested Sauces: Bearnaise Sauce, Curry Sauce, Hollandaise Sauce, Sate Sauce or Tropical Sauce.

Hawaiian Chicken

2 x 1.5 kg chickens
salt and pepper
oil

Glaze

1 cup crushed pineapple
½ cup brown sugar
⅓ cup lemon juice
2 tablespoons soy sauce

Halve chickens. Season with salt and pepper. Brush with oil and place on medium hot griller with skin uppermost for 20 minutes. Turn and cook the other side for 15 minutes. Turn, brush with glaze on both sides and cook until chicken is tender, basting frequently. Barbecue time about 40–50 minutes.

Serves 8

Tarragon Tempters

chicken drumsticks (2 per
 person)
melted butter
lemon juice
dried tarragon
paprika to taste

Brush drumsticks with melted butter and arrange on grill over a good hot fire. Barbecue about 5 minutes, turn and sprinkle with lemon juice and dust with tarragon and paprika. Repeat turning, sprinkling and dusting until drumsticks are cooked and juice runs clear. Serve with small paper napkins wrapped around bone. Barbecue time about 20–25 minutes.

Tarragon Tempters

Spiced Barbecued Chicken

Spiced Barbecued Chicken

2 x 1 kg chickens

Butter Baste
125 g butter
1½ teaspoons salt
freshly ground black pepper
juice 1 lemon or 2 limes
¼ cup tomato sauce
few drops Tabasco sauce
1 teaspoon dried thyme
1 clove garlic, crushed

Wash and dry chickens and split in half. Melt butter in a saucepan, add remaining ingredients and stir. Brush chickens with butter baste and place on barbecue grill, skin side up, over a hot fire. Barbecue 20 minutes each side, brushing with butter baste occasionally. Barbecue time about 30–40 minutes.

Serves 4–6

Chunky Chicken Cognac

4 breast or 8 thigh fillets
100 g butter or a good
  splash of oil
150 mL cognac
lettuce leaves, washed and
  dried

Skin fillets and cut into 2 cm pieces. If using breast and thigh fillets, don't mix together as the cooking time for each is a little different. Melt butter in cast iron pan or wok over a good hot fire taking care not to let the butter burn. Add chicken and toss gently for about 5 minutes; thigh fillets take a minute longer. When almost cooked, remove pan from heat, pour over warmed cognac, ignite and toss until flame dies away. Serve piled on a bed of crisp, green lettuce leaves or with rockmelon slices. Barbecue time about 5 minutes.

Serves 4

Chicken Teriyaki

1.5 kg chicken pieces

Marinade
½ cup soy sauce
¼ cup honey
1 clove garlic, crushed
½ teaspoon ground ginger

Combine soy sauce, honey, garlic and ginger and marinate chicken pieces for 2–3 hours. Drain, reserving liquid, and barbecue chicken until tender. Turn and brush frequently with marinade. Barbecue time about 20–25 minutes.

Serves 6

Brandied Chicken

Chicken Teriyaki

Brandied Chicken

6 ripe peaches, stoned and
*   halved*
6 ripe apricots, stoned and
*   halved*
2 x 1.5 kg chickens

Marinade
125 g butter, melted
¼ cup lemon juice
¼ cup brandy
⅓ cup brown sugar

Allow fruit to steep in marinade for at least 1 hour. Set to keep warm near griller. Place chickens on griller over direct hot heat. Brush with extra melted butter. Grill for 20 minutes, turn and grill for 15 minutes, turn again. Brush chicken all over with marinade frequently. Serve chicken with warmed fruit. Barbecue time about 35–40 minutes.

Serves 4–6

Chicken Kebabs

Chicken kebabs are best made with skinned breast meat, cooked over a medium fire and basted just before serving. Spicy chicken kebabs can be marinated before barbecuing for additional favour. It is important that pieces are cut the same size and the heat is controlled during cooking time.

Kids love kebabs
Hungry young mouths don't like to wait around too long! To keep them busy, ask them to make up their own kebabs, choosing their meat, vegetables and fruits. They will have fun and the food will be nutritious.

Chicken Kebabs. Use vegetables and/or fruits of your choice

Chicken with Pineapple and Orange

*fresh chicken breast fillets,
cut into 3 cm pieces*
*fresh pineapple pieces, cut
in 3 cm triangles
(pineapple should be a
little on the unripe side)*
*orange or mandarin
segments, about same
size as pineapple pieces*
Tropical Sauce (see recipe)

Thread chicken, pineapple and orange or mandarin segments alternately on skewers, allowing about 3 pieces of each per skewer. Barbecue over a medium fire. Brush with Tropical Sauce when almost cooked. Barbecue 1 minute more and serve accompanied with more sauce for dipping. Barbecue time about 15 minutes.

Chicken with Onion and Capsicum

fresh chicken fillets, skinned
white onions
red and green capsicums
*Tropical Sauce or
Peppercorn Butter (see
recipes)*

Cut chicken breasts into 3–4 cm pieces, quarter onions and cut capsicums into pieces same size as the chicken. Thread alternately on skewers for colour (allow 2 skewers per person) and cook over a medium fire. Just before removing from barbecue, brush with Tropical Sauce or Peppercorn Butter. Serve with more sauce for dipping, or extra Peppercorn Butter. Barbecue time about 15 minutes.

35

Chicken and Mushroom Kebabs

fresh chicken breast fillets
   cut into 3–4 cm portions
fresh field mushrooms cut
   into same-sized pieces
melted butter
dried tarragon

Allow about 4 pieces each of chicken and mushroom per skewer. Thread chicken and mushroom pieces on skewers alternately then barbecue over a medium fire. Just before serving brush with butter and tarragon. Barbecue time about 15 minutes.

Minted Turkey Drumsticks

8 same-sized turkey
   drumsticks
300 g mint jelly, melted

Barbecue drumsticks over a medium fire, controlling temperature. Turn frequently. Just before end of cooking time, brush with melted mint jelly. Cook 1 minute more and serve on a platter with rest of sauce and plenty of napkins. For a milder mint favour, add a little water to melted mint jelly. Barbecue time about 30–40 minutes.

Serves 4–6

Barbecued Turkey Breast

1–1½ kg turkey breast fillet,
   skinned and boned
250 g cranberry sauce
chilli sauce to taste

You can buy whole buffet breast of turkey or whole fillet of turkey breast. Bone as you would a chicken breast by cutting straight down each side of breast bone. This produces 2 full fillets of turkey. Remove wings and use separately. The leftover bones make great stock.

Place fillet in lightly greased wire basket and barbecue 30–40 minutes over a medium to hot fire. Control heat carefully. Serve sliced into 2 cm thick portions with cranberry and chilli sauces mixed to your taste. Barbecue time about 30–40 minutes.

Serves 6–8

Sate Chicken

Sate Chicken

fresh chicken fillets
Sate Sauce, bought or
   homemade (see recipe)

Cut the chicken fillets into slightly smaller pieces than for kebabs — about 2 cm square. Thread on skewers and cook over a medium fire, basting and turning continually. Brush with Sate Sauce and serve hot. Barbecue time about 10–15 minutes.

Duck Halves in Baskets

1.5 kg duck, defrosted if
   frozen

Wash and dry duck and split in half. Arrange in greased wire basket and barbecue over medium fire until tender.

Start cooking skin side down to crisp. After 10 minutes turn occasionally. Two-thirds of barbecue time should be skin up. Just before serving brush with your favourite sauce if you wish, though this is not necessary. Serve in baskets with sweet mango chutney or more of your favourite sauce. Barbecue time about 1 hour.

On the spit

Rotisserie cooking will impress the guests, but make sure that all the heat doesn't disappear into your neighbour's garden. The food on the spit cooks more quickly and evenly if you use reflected heat. So fit reflectors (baking sheets will do) to your barbecue. They should come to the top of the food.

Turkey Barbecue Kebabs

turkey breast fillets, skinned
and boned
dried apricots and dates or
capsicum, white onions
and cherry tomatoes
250 g cranberry sauce
dash chilli sauce (optional)

Cut turkey fillets into 3–4 cm cubes and thread on skewers alternately with dried fruits or with capsicum slices, onion quarters and cherry tomatoes. Allow 2 skewers per person. Barbecue over medium to hot fire. When nearly cooked, brush with cranberry sauce mixed with a dash of chilli sauce and serve. Barbecue time about 15 minutes.

Turkey Wings with Apricot and Chilli Sauce

8 turkey wings
Apricot and Chilli Sauce
* (see recipe)*

Barbecue wings over a medium fire turning frequently. Just before end of cooking time, brush with Apricot and Chilli Sauce. Barbecue 1 minute more, taking care that the sauce does not burn. Serve wings on a bed of lettuce with rest of sauce. Barbecue time about 20 minutes. Turkey wings are delicious served with fresh Passionfruit Sauce (*see recipe*).

Serves 4

Barbecued Turkey Breast

Turkey Wings with Apricot and Chilli Sauce and Minted Turkey Drumsticks

MEAT

Barbecuing is cooking, not creating: chewy steak won't be instantly transformed into juicy fillet on the barbecue. What you eat depends on what you buy in the first place. Buy aged or well hung meat and the better cuts. Poorer cuts need all the time they can get in the casserole in your kitchen. The quicker cooking of the barbecue demands the best meat. Beware of barbecue steak — there is no such cut. Buy the product not the price and take time to get to know your butcher. This way if you have a genuine complaint about quality, you have someone to take it to.

When preparing meat for the barbecue, trim off any excess fat just leaving a rim around the edges to prevent drying out during cooking. Take care to turn meat with tongs. A fork will draw out all those precious juices. Salt has much the same effect, so leave seasoning to later — and to your guests.

Most good cuts can be barbecued over a hot fire. Remember to control the heat by damping (charcoal) or moving food to the side (gas) as few people actually prefer burnt offerings. There's a great temptation with barbecuing, which is, after all, a social event, to enjoy the company and the conversation and forget the meat. Never turn your back on the barbecue: a watched fire won't get away from you.

The golden rule is that good meat doesn't need marinating to be tenderised. It is tender. Marinades offer extra flavours which broaden the barbecue repertoire in the same way as savoury butters and delicious sauces for dipping or pouring (see recipes).

Cut steak to different thicknesses for well done, medium or rare serves

Bercy, Garlic, Parsley Lemon, Chilli, Rosemary and Horseradish Butters (see recipes) are great with beef and so are the following sauces: Bearnaise, Hollandaise, and Digby's Special. Dab the meat with a little sauce just before serving and then present the rest warmed in a bowl or jug alongside.

Fillet of Beef with Bearnaise Sauce

1.5 kg whole tenderloin
Bearnaise Sauce (see recipe)

Prepare tenderloin by trimming off membranes, tendons and any excess fat. Barbecue over a good hot fire turning frequently. Warm Bearnaise Sauce in a pot at the side of the barbecue. Carve beef starting at thinner end of fillet following the technique described in Barbecued Whole Fillet (see recipe) and serve with warmed Bearnaise Sauce and fresh, crisp salads. Barbecue time about 30 minutes.

Serves 6

Fillet of Beef with Bearnaise Sauce in well done, medium and rare slices

Beef

One of the pleasures of barbecued beef is to have it cooked to perfection. For some people that will mean well done, for others medium, rare and blue for the rest. How on earth can the chef cope with all these requirements and serve everyone with hot beef at the same time? As with so many things in life, it's easy when you know how. With steaks, for example, cut them to slightly different thicknesses — you or your butcher can do this. The thicker cuts will still be rare when the thinner are well done with the bonus that you can readily identify by size which is which. With kebabs, place those to be rare on the grill a little later. As for quantities, remember the old rule of 250–300 g per person or allow a couple of kebabs a head.

Best quality Australian beef is unsurpassed on its own or served with horseradish, mustards, savoury butters and sauces. Marinating also adds zest to a beef kebab or steak.

Prime rib roast, whole fillet steak, kebabs and chops on the barbecue grill

Steak in Orange Sauce

2 kg skirt steak, sirloin or
  round, cubed

Marinade

¼ cup sugar
3 tablespoons vinegar
1½ cups fresh orange juice
1 tablespoon lemon juice
½ teaspoon dry mustard
2 beef stock cubes
cream

Caramelise sugar in a frypan over low heat. Stir in vinegar and orange juice. Cool. Add lemon juice and mustard and pour over cubed meat. Allow to marinate overnight. Remove steak and skewer. Place remaining marinade into a saucepan at the side of fire, add stock cubes and allow to simmer while steak is cooking over hot coals. Thicken sauce with a little cream and pour over meat to serve. Barbecue time about 15 minutes.

Serves 6–8

Stuffed Sirloin Steak

1 kg sirloin steak, 4–5 cm
  thick
1 onion, finely chopped
2 cloves garlic, crushed

125 g mushrooms, finely
  chopped
4 tablespoons red wine
2 tablespoons soy sauce

Slash fat edge of steak but do not cut into meat. Cut a pocket in lean steak near the bone. Combine onion, garlic and mushrooms and stuff into pocket. Mix together wine and soy sauce and brush over steak. Barbecue over a good hot fire, turning once. Brush occasionally with wine mixture. Slice and serve. Barbecue time about 15–20 minutes.

Serves 4

Carpetbag Steak

Rare, medium, or well-done?

No two guests like their steak quite the same. How can you serve everyone hot food at the same time and be able to tell which steaks are rare and which are well done? Like so many things, it is easy once you know how. Cut your steaks to different thicknesses. Thick for rare, a little thinner for medium and so on. The bonus is that all are ready at the same time and you can easily tell, by the thickness, which is which.

Steak 'n' Mushrooms Bourguignonne

1 kg rump steak, cubed
1 kg button mushrooms,
  whole

Marinade

½ cup red wine
1 teaspoon Worcestershire
  sauce
1 clove garlic
½ cup salad oil
2 tablespoons tomato sauce
1 teaspoon sugar
½ teaspoon salt
1 tablespoon vinegar
½ teaspoon dried rosemary

Blend marinade ingredients and allow beef and mushrooms to marinate for at least 2 hours. Alternate meat and mushrooms on skewer, starting and ending with mushrooms. Grill over medium heat, turning frequently and basting with remaining marinade. Barbecue time about 10–15 minutes.

Serves 6–8

Carpetbag Steak

1 kg piece rump steak, cut
  4 cm thick
freshly ground black pepper
1 dozen oysters, fresh or
  bottled
Anchovy Butter (see recipe)

Dust steak with freshly ground pepper and allow to sit for 10 minutes. Cut a pocket in steak with a sharp knife, insert oysters and seal with a small skewer or toothpick. Barbecue steak 5 minutes over hot coals, turn, top with a pat of Anchovy Butter and barbecue 5 minutes more. Carve on serving plate. Barbecue time about 10 minutes.

Serves 4

Barbecued Whole Fillet

Steak 'n' Mushrooms Bourguignonne (see page 40)

Sate Beef

rump steak
Sate Sauce, homemade (see
   recipe) or bought
cucumber, peeled and
   chopped into chunky
   portions

Cut rump steak into 1.5–2 cm cubes (this is smaller than for Beef Kebabs as the cooking time is shorter). Thread on skewers, about 4–6 cubes per skewer and cook over a good hot fire for no more than 10 minutes. Control heat. While barbecuing, dab with Sate Sauce and turn continually. Serve with rest of sauce and chunky portions of cucumber. Barbecue time about 10 minutes (maximum).

Barbecued Beef Kebabs

rump steak
white onions
red and green capsicums

Cut rump steak into 3–4 cm cubes. If using small white onions, parboil 5 minutes. Cut larger white onions and capsicums into 3–4 cm slices. Alternately thread meat cubes, onion and capsicum slices on skewers and barbecue over a good hot fire turning occasionally to avoid burning for 5 minutes (rare), 10 minutes (medium) or 15 minutes (well done). Place 'rare' kebabs on barbecue 10 minutes after those to be well done. Just before the end of cooking time, brush with sauce or simply serve with horseradish and mustards. Mushrooms are also tasty with barbecued kebabs. Barbecue time about 10–15 minutes.

Prime Rib Roast

1 kg prime rib roast

Ask your butcher to cut rib roast into individual prime rib cutlets, or cut them yourself. Barbecue over a good hot fire for 15 minutes (well done), 10 minutes (medium), and 5 minutes (rare) turning once. Place the 'rare' cutlets on grill later than those to be well done. Just before end of cooking time, brush cutlets with sauce if you want.

Ribs can be served with style standing or as individual cutlets with horseradish and a range of mustards or a warmed sauce such as Bearnaise (*see recipe*). Barbecue time about 10–15 minutes.

Serves 4

Barbecued Whole Fillet

1.5–2 kg whole tenderloin

Trim membranes, tendons and any excess fat. Barbecue whole over a good hot fire turning frequently as this will allow the fillet to baste in its own juice. When cooked, carve into 1–2 cm thick slices starting at the thinner end — which will be well done. As you continue carving you will notice that the thicker portion of the fillet will be rarer — so off one fillet you can present well done, medium, rare and blue beef.

Serve with horseradish sauce and your choice of mustards. Slices of whole fillet look very attractive on thin slices of French bread. Barbecue time about 30 minutes.

Serves 6–8

Stuffed Rolled Steak

1 kg skirt steak, cut in 1–2
  pieces
1 teaspoon meat tenderiser
2 tablespoons French
  mustard
3 cups bread cubes
½ cup onion, chopped
½ cup celery, chopped
125 g butter, melted
bottled Italian salad
  dressing

Score meat on both sides and rub with tenderiser. Spread mustard on one side of steak. Combine bread cubes with onion and celery, add melted butter and spread over steak on mustard side. Roll up and lace with string. Attach to spit and roast over medium coals until cooked basting frequently with salad dressing. Barbecue time 30 minutes.

Serves 6

Lamb

There's a lot more to barbecuing lamb than the traditional chop. The boned leg, laid flat and cooked in a wire barbecue basket and served with minted jelly, or stuffed, rolled and spit-roasted, or diced and served as sate brings gourmet flavours into the garden. So do rack of lamb or loin which look spectacularly when you want to make an impression. Lamb doesn't need to be well done over the barbecue, many people prefer theirs juicy and slightly pink. With rack of lamb you can cater for both by varying cooking times: place portions to be 'rare' on barbecue last.

Mint, rosemary and garlic are always great with lamb whether as herbs or sauces. Other flavours that provide mouthwatering alternatives include Apricot Baste, Green Butter or Oriental Sauce (*see recipes*).

Buying a Side of Lamb

When buying a side of lamb, ask your butcher to cut it for you in the following way:
☐ Cut off the leg at the end of the loin.
☐ Cut the shoulder and forequarter in one piece.
☐ Cut the short loin section.
☐ Remove the breast bone.
☐ Cut through the rib bones as close to the back bone as possible.

This gives you a leg and chump section which you can separate and serve as chops and a roast. The shoulder and forequarter portion is also ideal for roasting. Joint the loin and use as chops or barbecue. The ribs, cut this way, make delicious barbecued spareribs. Bone the meaty fillet called the 'cutlet eye', which is attached to the back bone, and use as is.

Barbecued Boned Leg of Lamb

1 large leg of lamb, boned
2–3 sprigs fresh mint
250 g jar mint jelly

Ask your butcher to bone the leg of lamb. Lay it flat and carefully remove sinews. Make 2–3 incisions in meat and insert mint. Place lamb flat in lightly greased wire basket and barbecue over a good hot fire. Turn regularly and control temperature. When nearly cooked, melt mint jelly. Carve in slices, brush with mint jelly and serve. Barbecue time about 30 minutes.

Serves 6–8

Lamb Spareribs

1 rib section
Digby's Special Sauce (see
    recipe)

Prepare rib section by removing skin or barbecuing half on/half off. If you leave on, cut through skin down the rib bone to allow excess fat to drain during cooking.

Place ribs on barbecue over a good hot fire, skin down to crisp first. Turn constantly, but two-thirds of cooking time should be with the skin up. Control temperature. Just before removing from fire, heat Digby's Special Sauce and baste spareribs.

Slice into individual spareribs and serve with plenty of sauce and napkins. As they say: the nearer the bone the sweeter the meat. Barbecue time about 20 minutes.

Serves 3

Rolled Kebabs

750 g lean lamb, minced
    twice
2 medium-sized onions,
    finely chopped
salt and pepper
3 egg yolks
pinch saffron
pinch cinnamon
pinch cumin

Combine lamb, onions, salt and pepper. Allow to stand 30 minutes. Add remaining ingredients and beat with a wooden spoon until mixture is very light. Divide into 6 portions and shape meat into sausage-like shapes, 5 cm in diameter, around skewers. Place over medium hot coals, turn frequently. The kebabs should be crisp outside, tender and juicy inside. Barbecue time about 5–10 minutes.

Tangy Lamb Cubes

½ kg cumquats
1 glass sherry
2 tablespoons sugar
1 kg lamb, cubed

Marinade
½ cup oil
½ cup orange juice
1 glass sherry
1 tablespoon
    Worcestershire sauce
salt and pepper

Simmer cumquats in sherry and sugar over low flame for 10 minutes. Cool in liquid. Combine marinade ingredients and steep lamb in marinade for at least 2 hours. Skewer lamb alternately with cumquats and add juice from fruit to marinade. Baste frequently. Cook over medium heat. Barbecue time about 10–15 minutes.

Serves 6

Stuffed Leg of Lamb

1 large leg of lamb, boned
juice 1 lemon
4 cloves garlic, crushed
    (optional)
freshly ground black pepper
125 g lamb, minced
1 onion, chopped finely
½ cup rice
pinch salt
pinch cinnamon
2 tablespoons finely
    chopped fresh parsley
1 tablespoon finely
    chopped fresh mint
1 egg yolk

Baste
4 tablespoons oil
4 tablespoons lemon juice
2 teaspoons rosemary

Lay lamb out flat on a board and brush with lemon juice, sprinkle with crushed garlic if using, and black pepper. Allow to rest while preparing stuffing. Heat minced lamb. Add onion, rice, salt and cinnamon. Saute until cooked. Add parsley and mint and remove from heat. When cool, stir in egg yolk and spread mixture over lamb. Roll up tightly and roast on spit over medium fire. Combine baste ingredients and brush occasionally as it cooks. Barbecue time about 2 hours, but test with a meat thermometer.

Serves 6–8

Note: If spit is not available, lamb may be wrapped in foil that has been coated with some of the basting mixture. Turn frequently and open foil and brush from time to time with baste. For the last 10 minutes of cooking time, unwrap lamb and allow to brown.

Shish Kebab

1 kg lamb, cubed
red and green capsicums
onions, cut in thick slices

Marinade
½ cup oil
¼ cup lemon juice
1 tablespoon salt
1 teaspoon allspice
1 teaspoon cumin
1 teaspoon crushed cloves
pepper
2 cloves garlic, crushed
½ cup onion, grated

Prepare marinade by mixing all ingredients well. Steep cubed meat overnight in the marinade, turning occasionally. Skewer meat alternately with chunks of green and red capsicum and thick onion slices. Brush with oil occasionally during cooking time. Cook over medium heat. Barbecue time about 10–15 minutes.

Serves 6

Shish Kebab. A variation includes shallots and sprinkling dried parsley over the marinating kebabs

Minted Lamb Kebabs

1 large leg of lamb, boned
dried apples
250 g jar mint jelly

Cut leg into 2–3 cm cubes and thread on skewers alternately with apples beginning and ending with lamb. Barbecue over a good hot fire, controlling the temperature and turning occasionally. When cooked, dab with melted mint jelly and serve hot.

Serves 8

Sate Lamb

1 large leg of lamb, boned
Sate Sauce (see recipe)

Sate lamb is delicious, so allow about 3 skewers per person. Cut lamb into 2 cm cubes — these are slightly smaller than for kebabs. Thread about 6 pieces on each skewer and cook over a good hot fire for 10–15 minutes basting continually with Sate Sauce and turning. Serve with bowl of warmed Sate Sauce and fresh fruit such as watermelon or pawpaw slices. Barbecue time about 10–15 minutes.

Serves 8

Rack of Lamb

end rack of 6 cutlets
½ cup Grand Marnier

Remove skin and fat from end rack and make an incision between cutlets so they will be easy to cut through and serve when cooked. Place rack in lightly greased wire basket. Barbecue over a good hot fire, controlling temperature carefully and turning occasionally, taking care that lamb does not burn. Warm Grand Marnier on side of barbecue. Arrange rack on warmed flameproof serving platter, pour over Grand Marnier and ignite. Cut into individual cutlets and serve. Barbecue time about 40 minutes.

Serves 4–6

Barbecued Loin of Lamb

1 short loin section
rosemary sprigs or dried
* rosemary leaves*
2 cloves garlic, peeled and
* cut into slivers*

Ask your butcher to cut and joint the loin for you. Skin and remove flap and excess fat. Make an incision between the chops and insert a sprig of rosemary and a sliver of garlic. Place loin in lightly greased wire basket and barbecue over a good hot fire, carefully controlling the temperature. When cooked, cut into individual chops and serve with mint sauce or jelly or other favourite lamb sauces. Barbecue time about 30 minutes.

Serves 2

Pork

Well done but not overdone is the rule for pork, so patience and care are required. Keep bastes and sauces free of fat because pork is such a rich meat. It goes well marinated in fruit flavours such as the Apricot Baste or served with sauces such as Plum, Plum and Chilli, Red Currant, or Sweet and Sour (see recipes).

The usual 'buy the best' rule applies. Ask your butcher about the 'new-fashioned pork' which offers alternative cuts of pork without excess bone or fat (excluding spareribs). Packs with a variety of different 'new-fashioned pork' cuts are also available.

When cooking spareribs, barbecue whole (this keeps the meat moist) and cut into individual serving portions when cooked. The same applies to the rack of pork. For kebabs, use a boned leg of pork as this gives you lots of meat with very little wastage.

Ham steaks are popular on the barbecue with their perennial partner — pineapple. Be adventurous and try some other fruits in season such as avocado, pawpaw or watermelon for a little variety. Ham steaks will cook in minutes as they are really just heating through. Watch carefully to make sure they don't burn and that glazes or sauces don't catch.

Barbecued Ham

1 large ham (about 3 kg)
* with rind removed*

Baste
1 tablespoon cinnamon
1 tablespoon mustard
1 tablespoon ground ginger
½ tablespoon crushed
* cloves*
1 glass whisky
2 tablespoons brown sugar
1 tablespoon golden syrup
½ cup wine vinegar
pineapple juice

Mix first 5 baste ingredients in a glass jar and allow to steep for 1 hour. Mix well with remaining ingredients and add sufficient pineapple juice to make 600 mL. Shake mixture each time before basting the spitted ham. The outside fat of ham will char black, but don't let it burn. Allow to cook for about 1 hour. Remove charred fat and allow to turn for another 10 minutes using up remainder of baste.

Serves 10–12

Control the heat

Flame does not cook meat, it burns fat. The secret of barbecued food is to control the heat: by damping charcoal or by moving food to one side with gas. When damping, sprinkle water carefully, just to reduce the temperature. Don't overdo it. If your grill is very close to the coals, it may be better to move food to one side while you damp down.

Pineapple Spareribs

Whole Loin of Pork

whole loin of pork, jointed
apple slices, dried or fresh
  brushed with lemon juice
  to prevent browning
apple sauce, bought or
  homemade

Ask your butcher to joint the loin of pork for you. Remove skin, all fat and flap. Cut between chops and insert dried or fresh apple slices. Barbecue over a good hot fire controlling temperature and turning about halfway through cooking time. When ready, cut individual chops and serve with salt and pepper to taste and apple sauce. Barbecue time about 30–40 minutes.

Serves 3

Pineapple Spareribs

2 kg pork spareribs
2 tablespoons French
  mustard
1 tablespoon salt
1 large tin pineapple slices
2 tablespoons honey
2 tablespoons vinegar

Brush ribs with mustard, sprinkle with salt and set aside. Mix juice from pineapple with honey and vinegar and simmer briefly. Place ribs, bone side down, on grill over low coals and brush frequently with glaze. Grill for 20 minutes, baste and turn for 15 minutes. Turn meat over again. Spike meat with toothpicks and pineapple slices. Brush frequently wirh glaze until meat is well done. Barbecue time about 40 minutes.

Serves 8

Ham Steaks

4 ham steaks, 2 cm thick
small can pineapple chunks
  or fresh pineapple cut
  into chunks

Marinade
½ cup tomato sauce
2 tablespoons brown sugar
2 tablespoons French
  mustard
1 tablespoon
  Worcestershire sauce
1 tablespoon lemon juice

Combine marinade ingredients. Slash fat edges of ham and allow to steep in sauce at least 1 hour, turning frequently. Drain. Barbecue over medium heat 4 minutes each side. Top with pineapple chunks and serve. Barbecue time about 8 minutes.

Serves 4

Ham Steaks

Pork Spareribs

1 rib section
Plum and Chilli Sauce (see
   recipe)

Ask your butcher to cut you the rib cage section, that is the eye cutlet and the ribs. Skin ribs and keep for crackling. Place ribs on barbecue and cook on hot fire turning regularly and controlling temperature. Baste at the finish with warmed Plum and Chilli Sauce. Slice and serve indvidual spareribs with more sauce and plenty of napkins. Barbecue time about 15-20 minutes, depending on size.

Serves 4

Note: The meaty section left after the ribs have been cut will take about 30 minutes more to cook.

Rack of Pork with Grand Marnier

rack of pork of 4 cutlets
150 mL Grand Marnier

Trim skin and remove fat, keeping skin for crackling. Make an incision between cutlets. Barbecue pork over a good hot fire turning occasionally. Cooking time will depend on the size of the cutlets. When pork is nearly cooked, warm Grand Marnier. Arrange pork on flameproof serving dish, pour over Grand Marnier and light. (This looks spectacular at night!) When flame dies down, carve into individual cutlets and serve. This dish is also good with cognac.

   For crispy crackling, rub a little oil and salt on skin, place in a wire basket and cook, skin to the coals, for 20-30 minutes. Turn occasionally, starting when pork is about half-done. Barbecue time about 40-50 minutes.

Serves 4

Pineapple Pork Kebabs

3 kg leg of pork, boned
fresh pineapple, cut in 2 cm
   thick slices
Tropical Sauce (see recipe)

Cut pork into 3-4 cm cubes and pineapple into 3 cm triangles. Thread pork and pineapple pieces alternately on skewers beginning and ending with pork. Barbecue over a good hot fire controlling temperature and turning occasionally. When nearly cooked, brush with Tropical Sauce and serve. Barbecue time about 15-20 minutes.

Serves 6-8

Barbecued Pork Kebabs

3 kg leg of pork, boned
dried fruits such as apricots,
   dates, apples
Plum and Chilli Sauce (see
   recipe)

Slice off just enough pork to make your kebabs. Keep remainder for roasting or freezing.

   Cut pork into 3-4 cm cubes and thread on skewers alternating with dried fruits for colour. Begin and end with pork pieces. Barbecue over a good hot fire turning occasionally and controlling temperature. When nearly cooked, brush with Plum and Chilli Sauce and serve. Barbecue time about 15-20 minutes.

Serves 6-8

Hawaiian Ham Kebabs

500 g thick ham steaks,
   cubed
1 fresh pineapple, sliced
80 g melted butter

Glaze
1 cup brown sugar
½ cup honey
½ cup orange juice

Cut ham steaks and pineapple slices into 3 cm cubes. Combine glaze ingredients and warm. Marinate ham in warm glaze for a few minutes. Drain, retaining glaze. Thread ham and pineapple cubes alternately on skewers. Barbecue over low heat, basting alternately with melted butter and glaze. Turn frequently. Barbecue time about 5 minutes.

Serves 6

Sate Pork

3 kg leg of pork, boned
Sate Sauce (see recipe)

Cut boned leg pork into 2-3 cm cubes, slightly smaller than kebab-sized pieces. Thread about 6 pork pieces on each sate stick or skewer and barbecue over a good hot fire turning occasionally and controlling temperature. Brush with Sate Sauce throughout cooking time and serve with more sauce. Barbecue time about 15 minutes.

Serves 6-8

Crackling

To cook crackling without overcooking the meat, take the rind off the meat and cook the skin separately. For crispy, crunchy crackling, rub the skin with oil and salt and cook over medium-to-hot coals.

The Burger

The best burgers are made with the best meat. Select prime, lean meat and ask your butcher to mince it for you. Mix any seasonings in lightly; don't pound it all to a pulp. For barbecues, burgers should all be the same size so you can serve everyone together. A good size is that of an egg ring — about 2 cm thick and 7 cm across which will take 10–15 minutes to cook. Use egg and fresh breadcrumbs for binding and add seasonings to suit. Spicy burgers are tasty but children often prefer the standard flavourings.

For parties you can prepare all the patties in advance with waxed paper in between and store, covered, in the refrigerator. Then barbecue and serve with separate bowls of sliced tomato, beetroot, lettuce, pickles, sauces like Digby's Special, Hamburger or Jerez, mustards, mayonnaise, grated cheese and whatever else you fancy. This way your guests make their own burgers and everyone is happy.

The Hamburger

1 kg prime beef, minced
1 cup fresh breadcrumbs
2–3 eggs (depending on size), beaten
1–2 small onions, finely chopped
2 tablespoons chopped fresh herbs such as basil, rosemary, thyme or oregano, mixed to taste
Digby's Special Sauce (see recipe)

Combine all ingredients. Roll into 10 equal balls then flatten into patties about the size of an egg ring (about 2–3 cm thick and 7–8 cm across). Barbecue over a medium to hot fire 10–15 minutes, turning about halfway through. Just before the end of cooking time, brush with Digby's Special Sauce and serve with bread rolls or buns and everything else you need to make a great hamburger: German mustard, mayonnaise, pickles, shredded lettuce, finely sliced tomato, cooked onion rings . . . and more sauce. Barbecue time about 15 minutes.

Makes 10

Blue Cheese Burgers

1 kg minced beef
4 tablespoons chopped fresh parsley
10 hamburger buns, split and toasted

Filling

4 tablespoons crumbled blue cheese
1 tablespoon cream
4 tablespoons finely chopped onion

Mix beef lightly with parsley and divide into 20 patties on separate pieces of waxed paper. Combine filling ingredients. When required, place a spoonful of filling between two burgers, seal edges well and grill some 7 cm from coals for 6 minutes. Turn, sprinkle with salt and pepper and grill 5 minutes more. Slip burgers onto roasted buns. Barbecue time about 10 minutes.

Makes 10 burgers

Blue Cheese Burgers

The Hamburger (see page 49)

Food preparation

Try to prepare as much food as possible in advance. Choose foods that can remain in the refrigerator or freezer for a few days, so that once the guests arrive, only the barbecue items are left to cook.

Oriental Burgers

500 g beef, minced twice
1 teaspoon dried mint or 1
   tablespoon chopped
   fresh mint
½ teaspoon cumin
¼ teaspoon cayenne
1 egg

Blend minced beef with the mint, cumin and cayenne. Bind with egg and place mixture in the refrigerator for at least 1 hour before shaping into burgers. This burger may also be formed into long sausage shapes and served between frankfurter bread rolls if preferred. Cook over medium heat on both sides. Barbecue time about 10–15 minutes.

Serves 6

Gin Fizz Burgers

1 kg minced beef
1 tablespoon
   Worcestershire sauce
1 tablespoon tomato sauce
½ teaspoon salt
freshly ground black pepper
2 tablespoons sesame seeds
½ teaspoon dried basil
4 tablespoons gin

Mix all ingredients lightly, adding gin last of all. Grill burgers over hot coals 4–6 minutes on each side. Serve with a green salad sprinkled with toasted sesame seeds. Barbecue time about 10 minutes.

Makes 8 burgers

Minty Lamb Burgers

2.5–3 kg boned leg of lamb
2 onions, finely chopped
1–2 cloves garlic, crushed
2 tablespoons chopped
   fresh mint
1 teaspoon paprika
salt and pepper
3 eggs, beaten

To Serve
250 g butter
2–3 tablespoons chopped
   fresh mint
burger buns

Trim all skin and visible fat off lamb then cut into pieces. Mince, using a food processor or mincer. Avoid processing the lamb too finely.

Place mince in a bowl with all remaining burger ingredients and mix well. Cover and refrigerate.

Beat butter until soft. Add mint and beat again. Taste for mint flavour and add freshly ground pepper. Spoon butter onto a sheet of foil and roll into a log shape. Refrigerate until serving time.

Divide lamb mixture into 20 parts. With wet hands, shape each into a burger shape. Cook over glowing coals until done. Serve burgers topped with a thin slice of mint butter. Barbecue time 5–10 minutes.

Serves 10–12

Devilled Burgers

1 kg minced beef
2 eggs, beaten
½ cup chilli sauce or 1
   tablespoon Tabasco
   sauce
1 teaspoon salt
freshly ground black pepper

2 teaspoons French mustard
2 teaspoons horseradish
1 large onion, finely
   chopped
2 teaspoons Worcestershire
   sauce
10 hamburger buns

Combine all ingredients except buns. Shape into 10 equal-sized burgers. Cook over medium heat for 10 minutes. Turn and cook 5 minutes. Split buns, toast over coals and sandwich burgers into buns to serve. Barbecue time about 15 minutes.

Makes 10 burgers

Minty Lamb Burgers

Sausages

In the great outdoors, nothing beats the traditional barbie. Sausages have long been a barbecue favourite with children and adults alike. These days a wide range of traditional, continental and spicy sausages, such as curry, tomato and garlic, are available from butchers, specialty shops and delicatessen counters — so don't be afraid that the common sausage will be too dull for the up-to-date barbecue.

The perfect barbecued sausage should be parboiled first. This way it will be cooked on the inside and browned on the outside. Some shops will stock parboiled sausages for you. Otherwise, parboil them yourself by covering with water, bringing slowly to the boil and simmering 5 minutes. Drain, cool and store sausages overnight to let them settle and get cold. Parboiling cuts down the fat, the flaring and the cooking time. Don't be afraid to cut sausages to check if they are done. If you don't use parboiled sausages, make sure you prick them before barbecuing.

When catering, count on 2–3 sausages per person, remembering that cold sausages always make a great midnight snack. Serve sausages with traditional tomato sauce, mustards, Digby's Special Sauce (see recipe) and with thick slices of bread or crunchy breadrolls.

Weisswurst

This white herb sausage is delicious whole or cut in chunks, barbecued over a medium heat and served with German mustard.

Weisswurst Kebabs

weisswurst
dried fruits such as apricots,
  dates and apple

Skin sausage and cut into 3–4 cm thick slices. Thread on skewers alternating with dried fruits for colour. Barbecue gently over a medium heat turning occasionally. Serve with a mild flavoured sauce such as cranberry or German mustard. Barbecue time about 15 minutes.

Franks 'n' Fruit

cocktail frankfurts
dried fruits such as apricots,
  dates; apples
Digby's Special Sauce (see
  recipe)

Cut frankfurts into 3–4 cm thick slices and thread on skewers alternating with dried fruits for colour. Barbecue slowly over a medium heat, turning occasionally and controlling temperature. Serve with Digby's Special Sauce or a selection of mustards. Remember, frankfurts just need heating through. Barbecue time about 10 minutes (maximum).

Chipolata

Chipolatas need to be cooked gently, so parboil first then barbecue over a medium heat, turning frequently. Serve whole or sliced on skewers with mustards and sauces. They are a great favourite at sausage sizzles and children's parties, served hot or cooked in advance and served cold. Barbecue time about 10 minutes.

Bangers 'n' Buns

sausages, plain or flavoured,
  parboiled
crispy fresh breadrolls or a
  tank loaf cut into thick
  slices

Barbecue parboiled sausages over medium heat 10–15 minutes controlling temperature and turning to brown evenly all round. Serve with bread or rolls, buttered if you like, sauce and mustards to taste. Barbecue time depends on the thickness of the sausages and whether or not they are parboiled. Parboiled sausages will barbecue in about 10–15 minutes. Cut into them to make sure they are cooked.

Stuffed Sausages

good quality sausages, beef
  or pork, parboiled

Fillings
fresh oysters
asparagus spears
smoked oysters
banana slices
melted Parmesan cheese

Barbecue sausages over medium fire until cooked. Make a cut along the sausage, leaving about 1 cm uncut at each end. Insert selected fillings plus any others you wish to try. Barbecue time about 15 minutes.

Spice that sausage sizzle with variety

Many savoury sausages are now available and are excellent for barbecuing.
  Try some of the following:

Beef and Blackbean	Kransky
Beef and Tomato	Lamb Provencale
Blackbean and Honey	Pork and Bacon
Bratwurst	Pork and Apple
Chicken	Mexicana
Chicken Sate	Minted Lamb
Chicken Supreme	Peppercorn
Colonial Beef	Pork and Veal
Curry	Sate Beef
Garlic	Tomato and Onion
Hawaiian	Turkey and Chives
Italian Spicy	Turkey and Sage

Clockwise from top: Weisswurst Kebabs, Franks 'n' Fruit, Stuffed Sausages

SAUCES, BASTES AND BUTTERS

It's in the area of sauces that imagination is all. Follow these recipes, but adapt them to your taste. By all means mix your own sauces, but if you don't have time, don't hesitate to invest in some of the gourmet delights now found on the shelves of delicatessens and specialty shops. Some sauces are best served warm, so sit them in a pot alongside your barbecue where they can quietly heat through. Many dishes benefit by being brushed with sauce with a dabbing action just before serving. The rest of the sauce can be served in a bowl — or a gravy boat — alongside.

Adjust ingredients in these sauce recipes to suit your taste buds and the quantity you require. Leftover sauce can be stored in an airtight container in the refrigerator for a few days.

Savoury butters with herbs and spices can be made in advance and stored in the refrigerator. Mix together butter and herbs, roll in greaseproof paper into a log shape, then wrap tightly in freezer paper and aluminium foil. Store in the freezer and simply slice pats as required. Savoury butters are great with sizzling steaks and vegetables.

SAUCE IDEAS

This chart lists which sauce goes well with the barbecue recipes in this book. It is simply intended as a starting point. Let your own tastebuds be your guide.

The Food	Sauces	Bastes	Butters
Goes with anything on the barbecue	Bearnaise, Bechamel, Curry, Digby's Special, Hollandaise, Mushroom, Peanut, Sate		
Seafood	Avocado, Bearnaise, Bechamel, Caper, Curry, Digby's Special, Easy Garlic, Hollandaise, Mayonnaise, Mushroom, Peanut, Sate, Simple Seafood Butter Sauce, Spiked Seafood, Sweet and Sour		Anchovy, Basil, Bercy, Dill, Green, Horseradish, Parsley Lemon
Poultry	Apricot and Chilli, Avocado, Bearnaise, Bechamel, Digby's Special, Hollandaise, Mayonnaise, Mushroon, Oriental, Peanut, Plum and Chilli, Red Currant Sauce, Sate, Tropical	Chicken Pieces Marinade, Poultry Wine Baste, Paw Paw Baste, Apricot Baste	Garlic, Herb, Peppercorn
Beef	Barbecue, Bearnaise, Bechamel, Curry, Digby's Special, Espagnole, Hamburger, Hollandaise, Mushroom, Oriental, Peanut, Sate	Spanish Marinade	Anchovy, Basil, Bercy, Chilli, Horseradish, Oregano, Parsley Lemon, Peppercorn, Rosemary
Lamb	Bearnaise, Bechamel, Curry, Digby's Special, Hollandaise, Mushroom, Oriental, Peanut, Sate	Apricot Baste, Mint Marinade	Bercy, Garlic, Green, Horseradish, Oregano, Parsley Lemon, Peppercorn, Rosemary
Pork	Digby's Special, Peanut, Plum and Chilli, Red Currant, Sweet and Sour, Tropical	Apricot Baste, Spanish Marinade	Bercy, Chilli, Garlic, Horseradish, Parsley Lemon, Peppercorn, Rosemary
Vegetables	Bearnaise, Bechamel, Cheese, Hollandaise		Basil, Bercy, Dill, Garlic, Horseradish, Oregano, Parsley Lemon

Sauces, bastes and butters are an ideal accompaniment to barbecued meat and vegetables, poultry and seafood

Sate Sauce

½ cup sultanas
½ cup raisins
1 cup peanuts
2 tablespoons grated fresh
  ginger root
3 cloves garlic, crushed
1 tablespoon chilli sauce,
  more if you wish
1 cup white vinegar
½ cup sugar
5 tablespoons peanut butter
2 cups water

Finely chop sultanas, raisins, peanuts and ginger root and place in a saucepan with the rest of ingredients. Heat, stirring until sugar is dissolved. Simmer about 30 minutes, stirring occasionally.

Makes about 1.5 litres

Bearnaise Sauce

180 g butter
3 tablespoons vinegar
3 tablespoons dry white
  wine
8 black peppercorns,
  crushed
salt

2 tablespoons finely
  chopped shallots
1½ tablespoons finely
  chopped fresh tarragon
3 egg yolks

Melt butter, remove foam from the surface and cool to tepid.
  Combine vinegar, wine, peppercorns, salt, shallots and 1 tablespoon tarragon. Boil until reduced to 2 tablespoons. Strain and cool to room temperature. Add to egg yolks and whisk for 1 minute.
  Place the mixture in a double boiler over hot water and beat vigorously until thick and creamy. The base of the pan containing mixture should never be more than hand hot. Remove from heat and whisk in tepid butter, add a few drops at a time, until sauce starts to thicken, and thereafter in a very thin stream. Do not add sediment at the bottom of butter.
  Stir in remaining chopped tarragon.

Makes about 1 cup

Passionfruit Sauce

12 ripe passionfruit
1 cup water
½ cup sugar, to taste

Remove pulp from passionfruit and set aside. Heat water, add sugar and stir until dissolved. Add pulp, stirring continually. Simmer sauce to reduce and thicken. This sauce is delicious with turkey wings — simply baste wings just before removing them from barbecue. Unused sauce can be stored in an airtight jar in refrigerator.

Makes about 1½ cups

> **Dab to taste**
>
> Barbecue meals are even more mouthwatering when you simply dab with baste to taste just before cooking time is completed. Use a 5 cm wide paint brush to dab sauce or butter baste on the meat, chicken or seafood. This way you add flavour without making food look oily. It also prevents bastes and sauces which contain sugar from burning.

Simple Seafood Butter Sauce

125 g butter
good squeeze lemon juice
1 teaspoon chopped fresh
  parsley
1 teaspoon chopped fresh
  tarragon
1 teaspoon Worcestershire
  sauce
freshly ground black pepper
pinch salt (optional)

Melt butter and add remaining ingredients. Do not allow butter to brown. Use as a baste with all seafood.

Makes about ½ cup

Barbecue Sauce

1 onion, chopped
3 tablespoons oil
1 tablespoon
  Worcestershire sauce
½ cup tomato sauce

Combine all ingredients in a saucepan, bring to boil, cover and simmer 10 minutes, stirring occasionally. Allow to cool. Brush over meat before and during cooking. Suitable for rump, fillet, T-bone or any other tender steak.

Makes about 1½ cups

Curry Sauce

4 tablespoons oil or ghee
2 large onions, chopped
2 cloves garlic, crushed
2 tablespoons Madras curry
  powder
2 tablespoons flour
1 litre coconut milk,
  canned or fresh
cream (optional)

Heat oil, add onions and garlic and saute until tender. Add curry powder and flour and cook over gentle heat about 2 minutes stirring continuously. Gradually add coconut milk and simmer until sauce thickens. A little fresh cream can be used to soften the favour if wished.

Makes about 1 litre

Clockwise from top: Mint Jelly, Bearnaise Sauce, Cranberry Sauce, Sate Sauce, Passionfruit Sauce, Simple Seafood Butter Sauce and Barbecue Sauce

Plum and Chilli Sauce

550–600 g plum jam
chilli sauce
fresh cream (optional)

Heat plum jam in saucepan but do not boil. Add chilli sauce to taste. Use fresh cream to soften strength of chilli. Serve with pork and turkey.

Makes 2 cups plus

Apricot and Chilli Sauce

550–600 g apricot jam
chilli sauce
fresh cream (optional)

Heat jam in saucepan but do not boil. Add chilli sauce to taste. Use fresh cream to soften strength of chilli if desired. Serve with turkey.

Makes 2 cups plus

Digby's Special Sauce

600 mL tomato sauce
1 white onion, finely
* chopped*
1 garlic clove, crushed
¼ cup lemon juice
¼ cup claret
pepper
¼ cup brown sugar
½ cup Worcestershire sauce
½ cup chilli sauce
few drops Tabasco
1 teaspoon French mustard
3 tablespoons tomato paste
* (optional) or 2 ripe*
* tomatoes, blended*
1 cup water
½ teaspoon oregano
½ cup dry white wine

Combine all ingredients and simmer in a covered saucepan for about 1 hour, stirring occasionally. Do not boil. When making this sauce remember that the ingredients and their amounts can be altered to suit your own taste. Serve with almost anything that is cooked on the barbecue. Extra quantities can be frozen and stored until needed.

Makes 1.5 litres

Easy Garlic Sauce

185 g butter
2 tablespoons lemon juice
2 cloves garlic, finely
* crushed*

Melt butter taking care not to burn. Add lemon juice then garlic. Use as a baste for prawns or scallops.

Makes about 1 cup

Peanut Sauce

300 g shelled raw peanuts
3 fresh chillies or 3
* teaspoons chilli sauce*
3 cloves garlic
1 onion, chopped
100 mL peanut oil
½ cup water
1 tablespoon soy sauce
1 tablespoon brown sugar
2 tablespoons lemon juice

Combine nuts, chillies, garlic, onion and 50 mL oil and blend to a smooth paste, adding water when necessary. Heat remaining oil in frypan. Add peanut paste and stir well for about 3 minutes. Pour in rest of water and cook until sauce is thick and smooth. Stir in soy sauce, sugar and lemon juice. Taste to achieve desired flavour. Use with almost anything cooked on the barbecue.

Makes about 2 cups

Oriental Sauce

1 teaspoon grated fresh
* ginger root*
1 clove garlic, crushed
¼ cup soy sauce
1 tablespoon sherry
2 teaspoons sugar
2 teaspoons oil

Combine all ingredients and brush on meat before and during cooking.

Makes about ½ cup

Sauce Remoulade

1 large egg yolk, at room
* temperature*
pinch mustard
pinch salt
dash cayenne pepper
¾ cup salad oil, at room
* temperature*
1 tablespoon white vinegar
lemon juice
¼ teaspoon mustard
2 teaspoons finely chopped
* fresh parsley*
1 teasoon gherkin, chopped
pinch dried tarragon
6 anchovy fillets, finely
* chopped*

Make a mayonnaise by whisking together egg yolk, mustard, salt and pepper. Add oil drop by drop and then beat in remaining ingredients.

Makes about 1 cup

Mayonnaise (left) and Tartare Sauce

Mayonnaise

A very popular cold sauce with many exciting variations, one classic being Tartare Sauce. Mayonnaise blends particularly well with the flavours of chicken and seafood.

4 egg yolks
salt and freshly ground
  black pepper
1 teaspoon prepared
  mustard
250 mL vegetable oil
1–2 tablespoons white wine
  vinegar

Whisk egg yolks, salt, pepper and mustard together until thick, then gradually add the oil, drop by drop, whisking constantly until 1/4 cup has been incorporated. Add the rest of the oil in a thin steady stream and continue to whisk. Check the consistency occasionally and when the mayonnaise begins to thicken and whisking is difficult, add a little vinegar to thin down the sauce.

When all the oil is incorporated, taste and adjust the seasoning with salt, pepper and vinegar.

Makes 1 cup

Spiked Seafood Sauce

150 mL cream, slightly
  whipped
2 tablespoons horseradish
1 tablespoon finely snipped
  chives
dash Tabasco sauce

Whip cream slightly. Stir in horseradish until well blended. Add chives and Tabasco to taste.

Watch the salt

Go light on salt, it dries out food while cooking. Let your guests add their own salt to taste. If you do like to season foods, don't be heavy-handed. Try spices or herbs instead.

Tartare Sauce

1 cup Mayonnaise (see
  recipe)
60 g gherkin, finely diced
30 g capers, chopped
finely chopped fresh parsley

Combine all ingredients in a bowl and mix together until they have a smooth consistency. Tartare sauce can be served as an accompaniment to most seafood dishes whether hot or cold.

Store in a well-sealed jar, preferably glass, in the refrigerator for up to 10 days if homemade Mayonnaise was used, or for about one month otherwise.

Makes 1½ cups

Bechamel Sauce

This is excellent on its own or as a starter for other sauces.

2½ cups milk
1 small onion, cut in half
1 bay leaf
5 peppercorns
2 cloves
60 g butter
4 tablespoons flour
salt and pepper

Place milk, onion, bay leaf, peppercorns and cloves in saucepan and bring slowly to boil. Turn off heat, cover and let stand for 6–7 minutes. Strain, retaining milk.

Melt butter over low heat, add in flour and cook 2 minutes stirring continuously. Pour in strained milk slowly and bring almost to the boil stirring continuously. Reduce heat and cook a further 2–3 minutes. Add salt and pepper to taste.

Makes about 3 cups

Variations:

Cheese Sauce: Once sauce has thickened, remove from heat and add 1 cup grated tasty cheese, French mustard and more pepper to taste. Stir until cheese melts.

Mushroom Sauce: Add about 150 g mushrooms, sliced and cooked.

Chilli Sauce: Add about ¼ cup bottled chilli sauce or more to taste.

Mornay Sauce: Add ⅔ cup fresh cream and boil to reduce by about ⅓. Stir in ¼ cup grated Gruyere cheese, ¼ cup Parmesan cheese, 80 g butter and mix well.

Caper Sauce

1 cup mayonnaise
1 cup cream
2 tablespoons capers,
  drained

Combine mayonnaise and cream, add capers and serve with fish.

Makes about 2 cups

Hamburger Sauce

125 g butter, melted
½ cup oil
½ cup tomato sauce
1 teaspoon dry mustard
dash Worcestershire sauce
1 onion, grated
juice ½ lemon

Shake all ingredients well in a screwtop jar. Place near barbecue to warm slightly. Baste hamburgers with sauce before serving.

Makes about 2 cups

Sauce Jerez

250 g processed Cheddar
   cheese
1 cup dry sherry
1 tablespoon dry mustard
paprika, to garnish

Melt cheese in a double boiler and add sherry, a little at a time, stirring constantly. Add mustard and season to taste. Pour over fish, lamb chops or hamburgers. Sprinkle with paprika.

Makes about 2 cups

Red Currant Sauce

1 teaspoon salt
1 teaspoon freshly ground
   black pepper
1 tablespoon dry mustard
2 tablespoons brown sugar
1 cup vinegar
2 eggs
½ cup tomato sauce
1 cup red currant jelly

Combine salt, pepper, mustard and sugar. Stir in vinegar and simmer over low heat. Beat eggs lightly and add stirring constantly. When sauce has thickened add tomato sauce and red currant jelly, stirring continuously. Do not allow sauce to boil. This sauce is excellent with turkey, pork or grilled ham steaks.

Makes about 3 cups

Sweet and Sour Sauce

1 cup brown sugar
½ cup white wine vinegar
¼ cup orange juice
¼ cup lemon juice
1 tablespoon finely
   chopped capsicum
2 teaspoons cornflour
   mixed with a little water

Combine sugar, vinegar, juices and capsicum and simmer 5 minutes. Blend cornflour with a little water and stir in. Serve with pork, prawns or fish.

Makes about 1 cup

Avocado Sauce

3 ripe avocados
1 medium-sized onion,
   finely chopped
1 garlic clove, crushed
3 tablespoons lemon juice
1 tablespoon
   Worcestershire sauce
few dashes Tabasco
salt and pepper

Combine all ingredients and blend until smooth. Excellent with seafood.

Makes about 1 cup

Espagnole Sauce

This is a good basic sauce to which you can add many ingredients to create your own sauces.

60 g butter
1 small onion, finely
   chopped
1 small carrot, peeled and
   chopped
1 celery stalk, chopped
3 peppercorns
1 handful of parsley stalks
30 g bacon rashers or pieces
4 tablespoons flour
3 cups beef stock
dash Tabasco or
   1 tablespoon tomato
   paste

Melt butter in a heavy saucepan over gentle heat, add vegetables, peppercorns, parsley and bacon and cook until onion is golden. Add flour and cook and continue to stir until the roux is nice and brown. Add stock and bring to the boil stirring continuously. Add Tabasco or tomato paste and simmer gently about 30 minutes. Skim off any excess fat from bacon and strain through fine sieve. Excellent with beef or as a base for other sauces.

Makes about 3 cups

Tropical Sauce

1 cup salad oil
1 cup pineapple juice
1–2 tablespoons light soy
   sauce
2 tablespoons honey
1 teaspoon ground ginger
1 tablespoon cornflour
   blended with ¼ cup
   water

Combine all ingredients except the last two. Bring to the boil and simmer 5 minutes. Add cornflour and water mixture, stir until thickened then cook a further 3 minutes. Serve with pork and poultry.

Makes about 2 cups

Hollandaise Sauce

3 tablespoons white wine
    vinegar
5 black peppercorns
½ bay leaf
3 egg yolks
180–250 g unsalted butter
    cut into cubes and
    slightly softened
salt and white pepper
squeeze lemon juice
fresh dill, to garnish

Simmer vinegar, peppercorns and bay leaf together in a small saucepan until the mixture reduces to 3 teaspoons. Strain and set aside.

Place the egg yolks and 1 tablespoon of butter together in a heatproof bowl and whisk together, adding the flavoured vinegar. Place the bowl over a saucepan of gently simmering boiling water making sure the bowl does not touch the water.

Whisk the sauce constantly, adding the butter a little at a time. If the butter is added too quickly, the sauce may curdle. You may not need all the butter but the finished sauce should be a light, creamy colour, of foamy consistency and thick enough to coat the back of a metal spoon. Use immediately over barbecued meat or seafood dishes.

Makes about 2 cups

Bastes and Marinades

Good quality meat, fish or poultry does not need marinating before it is cooked. Marinades are used to tenderise cheaper cuts. Most marinades used as a meat tenderiser usually contain an acid such as lemon juice, vinegar or wine which tenderises the fibres; an oil to moisturise; and herbs, spices or seasonings for flavour.

However, marinating or basting can also be used with tender meat cuts to add spicy flavours. Dabbing with a baste or prepared sauce just before the end of cooking time is all that's required with good quality meats. You simply apply the sauce like a light glaze.

To marinate or not to marinate?

That is the question. Just remember when your product is good there is little need to marinate meat. Barbecue good meat or fish over a charcoal or heat bead fire letting the steam from damping replace lost moisture. Just before cooking time is completed, brush with sauce or baste.

Make up your own marinades to taste. Try chicken pieces in a simple white wine marinade with different spices for flavour

Paw Paw Baste

250 g ripe paw paw,
    chopped
2 tablespoons brown sugar
½ cup sherry
½ cup white wine vinegar
½ cup olive oil
1 tablespoon honey
½ teaspoon ground ginger

Combine all ingredients and simmer for 10 minutes. Use with poultry and allow to form a glaze while barbecuing.

Makes about 2 cups

Mint Marinade

1 onion, finely chopped or
    grated
2 cloves garlic, crushed
2 tablespoons chopped
    fresh rosemary
2 tablespoons chopped
    fresh mint
¼ cup wine vinegar
¼ cup boiling water
¼ teaspoon salt

Combine all ingredients in a glass jar and allow to steep for several hours before using. Use with lamb and baste as you barbecue.

Makes about 1 cup

Marinating fish

Apricot Baste

825 g can apricots
juice and grated rind 1
   lemon
2 tablespoons oil
1 teaspoon allspice
1 teaspoon salt

Puree apricots and syrup in a blender. Add remaining ingredients and simmer 10 minutes. An excellent baste for chicken, pork or lamb.

Makes about 2 cups

Chicken Marinade

2 cups dry white wine
½ cup salad oil
4 tablespoons light soy
   sauce or teriyaki sauce
2 tablespoons honey
2 teaspoons ground ginger
dash Tabasco or chilli sauce

Mix all ingredients together to taste. Add more soy sauce, honey or ginger if you want it spicier. Brush over chicken, marinate 1–2 hours or overnight in refrigerator. Drain, reserving marinade and barbecue over a medium hot fire. Brush chicken with marinade just before the end of cooking time and serve.

Makes about 3 cups

Spanish Marinade

1 onion, grated
2 cloves garlic, crushed
1 tablespoon dry mustard
1 cup dry sherry
1 cup soy sauce
½ cup brown sugar

Mix onion and garlic with mustard. Gradually add sherry, then soy sauce and sugar. Blend well. Marinate steak, spareribs or pork 1–2 hours at room temperature. Use remainder to baste while barbecuing.

Makes about 3 cups

Poultry Wine Baste

1 cup white wine
¼ cup olive oil
1 onion, grated
2 cloves garlic, crushed
1 teaspoon salt
2 teaspoons chopped fresh
   rosemary

Combine all ingredients in a saucepan and simmer 5 minutes. Baste chicken, or chicken pieces, before barbecuing.

Makes about 1½ cups

Chicken pieces brushed with Tandoori Mix

Savoury Butters

Savoury butters with herbs and spices can be made in advance and stored in the refrigerator. Mix together butter and herbs, roll in greaseproof paper into a log shape, then wrap tightly in freezer paper and aluminium foil. Store in the freezer and simply slice pats as required. Savoury butters are great with sizzling steaks and vegetables.

Anchovy Butter

Cream butter and add finely mashed anchovy fillets. Delicious with fish and veal.

Basil Butter

Pound plenty of fresh basil in a mortar and pestle. Cream into butter. Delicious with vegetables, excellent with fish and veal, superb on rice or pasta.

Bercy Butter

Cream butter with finely chopped shallots or chives. Great on steaks, chops, crayfish, prawns, vegetables and hot crisp bread.

Chilli Butter

Cream butter with Tabasco sauce and add a little chilli powder, but taste it as you mix. Very good with hamburgers and roast pork.

Dill Butter

Chop dill very finely and add to creamed butter. It is best to use only fresh dill for this to get the maximum flavour. A great dressing for fish and vegetable dishes.

Garlic Butter

Cream butter with fresh, crushed garlic and finely chopped parsley. Good on any meats that have been barbecued, lovely on baked potatoes and, naturally, great with hot bread rolls.

Green Butter

Pound parsley and chives in a mortar and pestle until liquid. Add to creamed butter until desired colour is achieved. Good with fish, roast lamb and oysters roasted in their shells.

Herb Butter

Cream butter with a mixture of herbs. Fines herbes from France can be bought in most delicatessens. Tarragon and chervil are especially good. If using dried herbs, steep briefly in a minute amount of boiling water to bring out the full flavour before creaming into butter. Fantastic with grilled poultry.

Horseradish Butter

To 125 g butter add 1 tablespoon French mustard and 1 tablespoon horseradish. Beat until light and fluffy. Excellent with grilled meats or fish and adds a zip to corn on the cob.

Oregano Butter

Soak dried oregano first in a very small amount of boiling water. Add to creamed butter. First rate with tomatoes, corn on the cob and lamb or veal.

Parsley Lemon Butter

Cream butter with very finely chopped parsley and lemon juice. Serve with grilled fish, vegetables, steaks, chops or liver.

Peppercorn Butter

Cream butter with freshly ground black pepper to taste and serve with poultry and meats.

Rosemary Butter

Chop fresh rosemary very finely then add to creamed butter with a sprinkle of lemon juice. Especially nice with lamb but good on any meat.

Parsley Lemon Butter is delicious with grilled meats and vegetables

BARBECUED VEGETABLES AND FRUITS

Whether it's a simple family get-together or a large gathering, what you serve with the cooked meat, seafood or poultry makes all the difference.

First of all there are the vegetables, like potatoes in foil or corn cobs which you can cook on the barbecue — or in the kitchen depending on time and space. Then come the fruits which can be served as an interesting and delicious dessert. You can try flambe fruits, fruit kebabs, or fruit wrapped in foil. Many of these fruits and vegetables can either be prepared well in advance, or can be small items which barbecue in a matter of moments.

Vegetables

Almost any vegetable can be cooked on the barbecue in foil providing you use a heavy-duty foil or double wrapping to prevent tearing. Wash vegetables, drain and dry, sprinkle with seasonings or simply a dob of butter then wrap and cook over medium heat until tender. Alternatively, if you are short of time or space, bake them in your oven at 180°C (350°F). A dish of water in the bottom of the oven will help keep the food juicy.

Vegetables can also be sliced into bite-sized pieces, skewered and served as kebabs with sauces like Bearnaise, Bechamel or Hollandaise and butters such as Dill, Basil and Parsley Lemon Butter (see Sauces, Bastes and Butter recipes).

Vegetable Kebabs

vegetables in season

Select a colourful variety of vegetables in season (tomatoes, onions, capsicums, broccoli, cauliflower, mushrooms), cut into equal-sized portions and thread alternately on skewers. Barbecue over medium heat, controlling the temperature and turning occasionally until tender.

Serve with Hollandaise or Bechamel (see recipes) or whatever sauce you are serving with the rest of the barbecue. Barbecue time depends on the vegetables. Remember you want them to be hot and crunchy rather than falling off the skewer.

Vegetable Kebabs

Foil Baked Potatoes

4 potatoes
4 tablespoons sour cream
4 teaspoons finely snipped
    chives

Wash potatoes, dry and prick with a fork. Lightly grease 4 squares of foil and wrap each potato. Barbecue about 45 minutes or until tender. When cooked, cut a cross on top, and squeeze potato gently to open. Top with sour cream and chives. Barbecue time about 45 minutes.

Serves 4

Cheesy Corn Kernels

3 cups corn kernels
60 g butter
½ cup cream
freshly ground black pepper
¼ cup grated Cheddar
    cheese

Make a pouch of foil. Fill with corn, butter, cream and pepper. Place pouch on grill over hot coals for 10 minutes. Remove from heat, sprinkle corn with grated cheese, close foil and return to side of griller for 10 minutes until cheese melts. Barbecue time about 20 minutes.

Serves 6

Potatoes Lorraine

8 oval potatoes
125 g butter, softened
1 packet onion soup mix

Scrub potatoes and cut lengthways into 3 slices. Blend soup powder with butter and spread on potato slices. Reassemble each potato on a piece of foil and close tightly. Bake over medium heat for 45 minutes, turning occasionally. Serve with meats. Barbecue time about 45 minutes.

Serves 8

Prepare ahead

Potatoes are terrific wrapped in foil and placed among the coals, but they can be cooked ahead of time and simply reheated on the barbecue. Another good idea is to blanch onions briefly in boiling water before barbecuing. They cook quicker; therefore it's less likely that they will be presented as charred offerings.

Potatoes Czarina

Potatoes Czarina

8 medium-sized, round
  potatoes, all same size
oil
300 mL sour cream
small jar red or black caviar
4 tablespoons finely
  chopped shallots

Scrub potatoes, dry, prick with a fork, brush with oil and wrap in foil. Barbecue over medium heat about 45 minutes, depending on size of potatoes. Unwrap carefully retaining foil, cut open and scoop out most of potato from shell. Mash potato smooth with sour cream and fold in half the caviar. Spoon back into potatoes, wrap again and reheat about 5 minutes. Serve topped with remaining sour cream, caviar and chopped shallots as an hors d'oeuvre or with barbecued fish. Barbecue time about 50–60 minutes.

Serves 8

Barbecued Sweet Potatoes

medium-sized sweet
  potatoes
butter
honey

Scrub potatoes, pat dry and place on foil. Top each with a knob of butter and a teaspoon of honey. Wrap and cook over medium heat until tender. Barbecue time about 45 minutes.

Watch that fire

Never turn your back on the fire — when you do, it can get away from you. Successful barbecuing is so easy with a little concentration (control that heat), and a bit of creative flair (otherwise known as constant taste testing).

Corn on the Cob

corn cobs
melted butter
salt and pepper or
*   seasoning salt*

Select tender fresh young corn with the husks still on. Carefully strip husks back and pull off the silky threads. Brush corn with melted butter and sprinkle with salt and pepper or seasoning salt. Pull husks back to original position and wrap in foil. Barbecue, turning frequently. When cooked, husks will be dry and cobs golden brown. If cobs have no husks or are frozen, treat in the same way, wrapping extra well in foil. Barbecue time about 20–30 minutes.

Skewered New Potatoes

Fill saucepans with salted water and sprinkle in a little dill. Thread 4–6 small potatoes on each skewer and immerse skewers in boiling water. Allow potatoes to cook at the side of barbecue over medium heat until tender. Dot each skewer with a little butter to serve. Barbecue time about 10–15 minutes.

Barbecued Mushrooms

40 g butter, melted
500 g mushrooms, washed
*   and trimmed*
salt and pepper

Cut 4 pieces foil, brushing one side with melted butter. Divide mushrooms between foil, sprinkle with remaining butter, season to taste and wrap securely. Barbecue until tender. Barbecue time about 10 minutes.

Serves 4

Hash Browns

potatoes, peeled and
*   parboiled 5–10 minutes*
butter, for frying
oregano
onions, finely sliced in rings
bacon pieces, fat removed,
*   cut into chunks*

Drain and cool parboiled potatoes and cut into slices 3–4 cm thick. At the barbecue, melt butter in frypan or on hotplate over medium heat and add oregano and potato slices. Turn continually. Add onion rings and bacon pieces, turning until cooked. Barbecue time about 10 minutes.

Barbecued Mushrooms. An alternative is to cook them with thinly sliced onion rings

Skewered New Potatoes

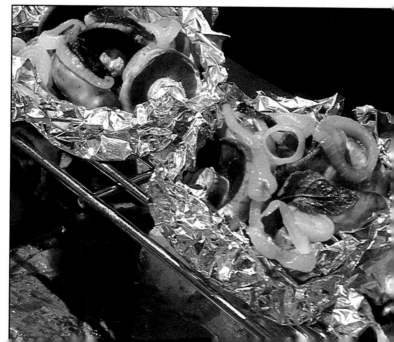

Stuffed Tomatoes

medium-sized tomatoes
fresh breadcrumbs
grated cheese
butter
dried tarragon

Slice tops off tomatoes, carefully remove pulp and blend with equal quantities of fresh breadcrumbs and grated cheese. Spoon mixture back into tomato cups, top with a dob of butter and sprinkle with tarragon. Wrap in foil packets and barbecue over medium fire to heat through. Barbecue time about 10 minutes.

Zucchini Squash

zucchini, sliced in 4 cm
   lengths
baby squash
melted butter, to baste

Choose zucchini and squash in different colours to make an attractive kebab. Thread alternately on skewers, brush with melted butter and barbecue over medium heat turning occasionally until tender. Cooking time will depend on the size of the vegetables. Barbecue time about 10 minutes.

Barbecued Corn Husks

Turn back husks of fresh corn and strip off silk. Put husks back into position and soak corn in a bucket of cold water for 1 hour. Shake off excess water and place over medium coals, turning occasionally. Cook until corn is tender. Strip off husks and serve with melted butter, salt and pepper. Barbecue time about 30 minutes.

Skewers

Make your own skewers that hold food in place when you turn your kebabs. All you need is stainless steel wire and a little time. Bend the wire into a hairpin shape about 20 cm long and 1.5 cm wide. You can make them while watching television.

The Barbecue Dessert

Seasonal Fruits

There's nothing quite like fruits in season for the barbecue dessert. Start with fresh fruit salad or foil-wrapped pears or apples with a little butter and brown sugar, perhaps even with a hint of rum, and heat through beside the barbecue until cooked. Bananas of course, don't even need to be wrapped first — their own skin does the job. Barbecued Fruit Kebabs (see recipe) make a delightful change and can be served on their own or with cream or ice cream. For a spectacular finish to a great meal out-of-doors try Flambe Fruit (see recipe).

Barbecued Fruit Kebabs

3 bananas, thickly sliced
2 apples, cut into chunks
1 pineapple, cubed
2 grapefruit, segmented
1 punnet
   strawberries, halved

Marinade
1 cup orange juice
¼ cup honey
2 tablespoons Cointreau
1 tablespoon brown sugar
1 tablespoon finely
   chopped fresh mint

Mix marinade ingredients together and heat gently to dissolve honey and sugar. Pour over prepared fruit and leave at room temperature 30 minutes. Thread fruit on skewers alternately for colour and barbecue until heated through. Turn and baste frequently. Barbecue time about 5 minutes.

Serves 6–8

Note: Barbecued Fruit Kebabs can be made with any fruits in season. Just keep colours and flavours in mind as you make your selection.

Barbecued Bananas

firm, green-tipped bananas

Barbecue bananas over medium heat turning frequently until skin turns black and flesh is tender. Barbecue time about 15 minutes.

Flambe Fruit

Flambe Fruit makes a great finish to a barbecue — especially at night. Use good quality fruits in season and cook in a large cast iron pan.

3 mandarins, peeled and
   segmented
4 pears, cut into slices same
   size as mandarin
   segments
1 cup overproof rum
200 g brown sugar
4 bananas, peeled and
   sliced
2 punnets medium-sized
   strawberries, hulled

Place mandarin segments and pear slices in pan (or on a large steel tray if you prefer). Add about 150 mL rum and stir in sugar thoroughly. Heat over barbecue then add banana slices. When juice starts to bubble add strawberries and stir gently. Remove pan from fire, warm remaining 100 mL rum, pour over fruit and ignite, stirring until flame dies down. Serve on a large platter with bamboo forks. Barbecue time about 5–10 minutes.

Serves 8–10

Flambe Fruit

SALADS

Salad making provides year-round opportunities for invention. Serve two or three with different dressings, or arrange prepared salad vegetables on a large platter with separate bowls of mayonnaise and dressings so your guests can help themselves. Salads don't have to be served with the main meal — try offering a platter of crudites for starters or as a prelude to cheese or dessert.

The amount of dressing you need for a salad doesn't always double when you double the recipe. For example, if you were to make double quantities of these salads, you would only need about half as much dressing again.

Salad dressing adds that extra zest to salads

Citrus and Mango Salad with Cream Dressing

1 lettuce
3 oranges, peeled and
   white pith removed
3 stalks celery, cut into
   8 cm pieces
450 g can mango slices,
   drained
1 cucumber, scored and
   sliced
6 shallots, finely sliced

Cream Dressing
¼ cup mayonnaise
½ cup cream
salt and pepper
2 tablespoons chopped
   fresh parsley
1 teaspoon French mustard
3 teaspoons orange juice
2 teaspoons lemon juice

Wash lettuce and arrange leaves on a serving plate. Segment the oranges. To make celery curls, slice the celery lengthways leaving one end uncut. Drop celery into iced water until it curls.

Arrange mango slices, orange segments, celery curls and cucumber slices between lettuce leaves. Garnish with shallots and refrigerate until ready to serve.

To make dressing, mix all ingredients well, stand 15–20 minutes before using and serve separately.

Serves 6–8

Chicken and Cheese Salad

3 cups torn endive
½ head lettuce, torn
3 hard-boiled eggs, peeled
   and sliced
½ cup sliced radishes
2 tomatoes, peeled, chilled
   and quartered
1 cup cooked chicken strips
1 cup Swiss cheese strips
¼ cup thinly sliced ham
¼ cup thinly sliced tongue
¼ cup thinly sliced salami
½ cup Italian dressing
anchovy fillets, to garnish

Combine endive, lettuce, egg and radish slices. Halve mixture. Place half endive mixture in row on square platter. Place tomato wedges next to endive mixture in row. Combine chicken and cheese strips and arrange in a row alongside tomatoes. Put rest of endive mixture beside chicken and cheese. Complete salad platter with combined mixture of ham, tongue and salami. Coat each row lightly with Italian salad dressing and garnish with anchovy fillets.

Serves 6

Mouthwatering salads can be prepared in advance

Fennel and Orange Salad

3 heads fennel
3 oranges
4–6 tablespoons Tomato
   Dressing (see recipe)
2 tablespoons chopped
   fresh parsley, to garnish

Trim fennel and slice thinly. Wash well and discard any discoloured slices. Cut both ends from oranges then cut off all rind and pith. With a small sharp knife, cut between membranes of oranges and free segments. Remove any seeds. Combine oranges, fennel and dressing. Cover, chill and serve sprinkled with parsley.

Serves 10–12

Tossed Green Salad

1 lettuce
1 cucumber, scored and
   sliced
1 green capsicum, sliced
6 shallots, chopped

Dressing
½ cup oil
¼ cup vinegar
½ teaspoon dry mustard
salt and pepper

Wash lettuce and tear into bite-sized pieces. Mix with remaining vegetables and chill. Shake dressing ingredients together in a screwtop jar, sprinkle over salad and toss. Serve immediately.

Serves 6

Beetroot Salad

Beetroot Salad

1½ tablespoons olive oil
1 tablespoon lemon juice
1¼ cups unflavoured
   yoghurt
1 clove garlic, crushed
¼ teaspoon salt
⅓ teaspoon white pepper
250 g cooked beetroot,
   diced
2 tablespoons finely
   chopped fresh parsley, to
   garnish

In a bowl, beat olive oil and lemon juice with a wire whisk. Add yoghurt, garlic, salt and pepper and stir until thoroughly blended. Fold in diced beetroot and transfer to a serving bowl. Sprinkle with parsley and serve.

Serves 4–6

Note: Canned baby beets can be substituted if fresh beetroot is not available.

Waldorf Salad

1½ cups diced apple
1 cup chopped celery
½ cup mayonnaise
¼ cup chopped walnuts
¼ cup seedless raisins
4 lettuce leaves
1 green apple, cored and
   sliced, for garnish
8 walnut halves, for garnish

Combine apple, celery, mayonnaise, walnuts and raisins and mix well. Pile onto lettuce leaves and garnish with apple slices and walnut halves.

Serves 4

Greek Salad

1 lettuce
8 cherry tomatoes
1 medium cucumber,
   peeled and roughly
   chopped

1 white onion, thinly sliced
6 radishes, topped and
   tailed
12 large black olives
100 g feta cheese, cubed

Dressing
3 tablespoons olive oil
1 tablespoon lemon juice
pinch dried oregano
fresh parsley, chopped, to
   garnish

Wash lettuce and tear into bite-sized pieces. Mix with remaining salad ingredients. Shake dressing ingredients together in a screwtop jar, sprinkle over salad and toss lightly together. Garnish with parsley.

Serves 6

Greek Salad

Spinach and Bacon with Avocado

Spinach Salad

1 bunch spinach
365 g can champignons,
    drained
3 rashers bacon, crisply
    fried

Dressing
½ cup oil
¼ cup white vinegar
1 clove garlic, crushed
salt and pepper

Wash spinach, remove stems and tear leaves into bite-sized pieces. Shake dressing ingredients together in a screwtop jar, sprinkle dressing over spinach and chill. Just before serving, fold through champignons, crumble bacon and sprinkle over top.

Serves 6

Exotic Flower Salad

1 large mango
1 tablespoon lemon juice
1 tablespoon salad oil
salt
125 g button mushrooms,
    finely sliced
freshly ground black pepper
1 large lettuce
1 tablespoon chopped fresh
    herbs
2 tablespoons pine nuts,
    toasted
60 g snow peas, topped,
    tailed and blanched
1 witloof, separated into
    leaves
1 quantity Creamy
    Vinaigrette Dressing (see
    recipe)

Peel the mango and cut a thick slice from each side of stone. Thinly slice these and set aside for the salad. Cut remaining flesh from stone and puree with lemon juice, oil and salt. Combine the mushrooms and pepper, and toss lightly.

Arrange lettuce leaves on a plate in a flower shape with the mushrooms in middle. Sprinkle over chopped herbs and nuts, arrange mango slices, snow peas and witloof on the plate. Drizzle Creamy Vinaigrette Dressing on top and serve.

Serves 6

Spinach and Bacon with Avocado

3 rashers lean bacon, finely
    diced
1 clove garlic, crushed
oil for frying
½ cup pine nuts
1 onion, sliced in rings
1 avocado, peeled, seeded
    and sliced
lemon juice
1 bunch English spinach,
    washed and drained
Vinaigrette (see recipe)

Heat oil and saute bacon with garlic. Add pine nuts and toss until golden. Drain and allow to cool. Separate onion rings and coat avocado with lemon juice to prevent it from browning. Place spinach leaves in salad bowl, add remaining ingredients and toss with dressing just before serving.

Serves 6

Farmhouse Salad

1 small red cabbage, finely
    shredded
salt
250 g belly pork
2 tablespoons oil
½ cup walnuts
finely snipped chives and
    chopped shallots

Dressing
2 tablespoons oil
1 tablespoon white wine
    vinegar
1 teaspoon dry mustard
salt and pepper

Sprinkle cabbage with a little salt, leave 1 hour, rinse and drain. Cut belly pork into squares, heat oil and fry until golden brown. Drain on kitchen paper and allow to cool. Shake together dressing ingredients in a screwtop jar. Combine salad ingredients, add dressing, toss well, and chill before serving.

Serves 6

Farmhouse Salad

Mushroom and Endive Salad

250 g mushrooms, thinly
    sliced
1 white onion, thinly sliced
1 cucumber, thinly sliced
1 green capsicum, thinly
    sliced
4 stalks celery, sliced
3 tomatoes, cut into wedges
1 bunch endive, washed
    and torn
1 lettuce, washed and torn

Dressing
3 tablespoons oil
1 tablespoon vinegar
1 teaspoon French mustard
1 clove garlic, crushed
    (optional)
salt and pepper

Prepare all vegetables and combine in salad bowl. Shake dressing ingredients together in a screwtop jar, sprinkle over salad and toss. Serve immediately.

Serves 6

Sour Cream Potato Salad

1 kg potatoes
4 tablespoons French
    dressing, bought or
    homemade (see recipe)
4 hard-boiled eggs,
    chopped
1 onion, finely chopped
½ cup finely chopped
    cucumber
½ cup finely chopped
    celery
1 cup mayonnaise
½ cup sour cream
1 tablespoon horseradish
    cream
salt and pepper
2 bacon rashers, crisply
    fried
1 tablespoon finely
    chopped fresh parsley

Cook potatoes in boiling water until they can be just pierced by a skewer. They must be still firm. Peel, cut into cubes and, while still warm, combine with French dressing. When cool, add eggs, onion, cucumber and celery.

Mix mayonnaise, sour cream and horseradish together and add to salad. Toss gently and season to taste. Crumble bacon and sprinkle over salad with parsley.

Serves 6

Green Salad with Dijon Mustard

3 cups torn spinach
½ head lettuce, torn
4 stalks celery, chopped
½ green capsicum, diced
1 cucumber, rinsed and
    sliced
2 tablespoons chopped
    chives
6 green olives, pitted and
    sliced, for garnish
1 avocado, peeled, seeded
    and sliced, for garnish

Dijon Mustard Dressing
1 tablespoon vinegar
2 tablespoons vegetable oil
1 teaspoon Dijon-style
    mustard
freshly ground black pepper

Wash and drain spinach and lettuce and combine with celery and capsicum. Place row of cucumber slices around edge of salad dish. Sprinkle chives over.

To make dressing, combine all ingredients in a screwtop jar and shake well. Toss spinach mixture with dressing, pile into centre of serving dish and garnish salad with olives and avocado slices.

Serves 6

Red Cabbage Nut Slaw

3 cups shredded red
    cabbage
1 cup shredded green
    cabbage
½ cup whole toasted
    blanched almonds

Base Dressing
2 tablespoons cream
1 tablespoon tarragon
    vinegar
1 teaspoon prepared
    mustard
¼ teaspoon garlic
    salt

Tahini Orange Dressing
2 tablespoons tahini
2 tablespoons water
juice and finely grated rind
    1 orange

Combine red and green cabbage, wash, drain and chill in refrigerator. Combine base dressing ingredients in a screwtop jar and shake well. Toss cabbage with dressing and ¼ cup almonds. Pile into salad bowl and top with remaining almonds. To serve, spoon over Tahini Orange Dressing.

Serves 6

Marinated Cucumber

2 medium-sized
    cucumbers, peeled and
    sliced
6 shallots, sliced, to garnish

Dressing
2 teaspoons salt
3 tablespoons white vinegar
3 tablespoons water
½ teaspoon sugar
¼ teaspoon paprika
¼ teaspoon freshly ground
    black pepper
½ clove garlic, crushed

Place cucumber slices in a shallow bowl. Combine dressing ingredients and pour over cucumber slices, tossing lightly to coat. Cover and chill in refrigerator for 3 hours. Garnish with sliced shallots to serve.

Serves 6

Avocado and Lettuce Salad with Mustard Seed Dressing

1 lettuce
2 avocados, peeled, sliced
    and sprinkled with juice
    ½ lemon
1 small cucumber, peeled
    and sliced
6 shallots, trimmed
alfalfa sprouts

Mustard Seed Dressing
2 tablespoons unflavoured
    yoghurt
1 tablespoon vegetable oil
2 teaspoons mustard seeds
1 teaspoon grated fresh
    ginger root

Wash and dry lettuce. Refrigerate 30 minutes until crisp then tear into bite-sized pieces. Place in salad bowl and top with avocado slices. Add cucumber and garnish with shallots and alfalfa sprouts.

To make dressing, combine all ingredients mixing until smooth. Just before serving pour over salad and toss.

Serves 8–10

Cooking with woks

Woks are wonderful! They can be easily used on a hotplate or grill and they don't require lots of heat to become quickly ready for use. Using a wok or heavy-based pan will open up a whole new world of barbecue cooking.

Clockwise from top: Avocado and Lettuce Salad with Mustard Seed Dressing, Red Cabbage Nut Slaw, Green Salad with Dijon Mustard

Brown Rice Salad with Tomato Dressing

2 oranges, segmented
2 cups brown rice, cooked
4 shallots, sliced
1 large red capsicum, diced
1 large green capsicum,
    diced
1 cup Tomato Dressing (see
    recipe)
salt
freshly ground black pepper

Cut rind and all pith from oranges. With a small sharp knife, cut between the membrane and flesh of each segment and free the orange flesh. Remove and discard any seeds.

Combine oranges, rice, shallots and capsicums. Pour dressing over and toss lightly. Season to taste. Place in a serving bowl, cover and chill until serving time.

Serves 10–12

Cucumber and Yoghurt Salad

2 cups unflavoured yoghurt
1 cucumber, finely
    chopped
4 shallots, finely chopped
salt and pepper
1 red chilli, finely chopped
grated rind ½ lemon, to
    garnish

Combine yoghurt with cucumber, shallots, salt and pepper and chili in a bowl. Serve chilled sprinkled with lemon rind.

Serves 6

Tabouli Salad

1 lettuce
½ cup shallots, finely
    chopped
2 cups finely chopped fresh
    parsley
½ cup finely chopped fresh
    mint
1 cup burghul (cracked
    wheat), soaked in water
    20 minutes and drained
¼ cup lemon juice
1 teaspoon ground allspice
    or pepper
salt and pepper
3 ripe tomatoes, peeled and
    finely chopped
¼ cup olive oil
black olives, for garnish

Finely slice lettuce leaves, leaving several whole as a base for the salad. Combine first eight ingredients in a bowl. Fold in tomatoes and olive oil. Arrange lettuce leaves on a platter or in a salad bowl, mound tabouli mixture on top, garnish with olives and serve chilled.

Serves 6

Turkey and Roquefort Salad

1 cup shredded lettuce
3 cups diced cooked turkey
1 cup diced celery
½ cup seedless grapes
½ cup toasted pecans,
    chopped
45 g Roquefort cheese,
    crumbled

Cranberry Dressing
250 g jar cranberry sauce
¼ cup dark soy sauce
1 small clove garlic, crushed
2 tablespoons lemon juice
2 tablespoons sherry
1 tablespoon vegetable oil

Combine lettuce, turkey, celery, grapes and pecans. Pile mixture into shallow serving dish. Crumble Roquefort cheese over top of salad.

Combine all dressing ingredients in a small saucepan and heat until well blended. Serve separately in a sauce boat.

Serves 6

Rice Salad with Prawns and Mussels

1 kg mussels
½ cup dry white wine
500 g freshly cooked king
    prawns
200 g rice
juice ½ lemon
6 tablespoons olive oil
freshly ground black pepper
1 small bunch fresh parsley,
    finely chopped
3 anchovy fillets, chopped
1½ lemons, sliced

Scrub mussels under running water to free shells of grit. Discard any open ones. Put them in a wide pan with wine and bring to boil. Remove with a slotted spoon as soon as they open. Shell approximately half of them, reserving the other half for decoration. Shell prawns.

Boil rice in salted water, drain it and run some cold water through it to separate grains. Season it with lemon juice, oil, plenty of pepper, parsley and anchovy fillets.

Just before serving, stir prawns into rice, reserving some for decoration. Arrange rice and prawns in a glass bowl and decorate with reserved prawns, mussels in shells and lemon slices. Serve very cold.

Serves 4

Savoury Rice Salad

375 g rice, cooked
1 red capsicum, finely diced
1 green capsicum, finely
  diced
2 stalks celery, sliced
6 shallots, finely chopped
6 water chestnuts, sliced
½ cup toasted almond
  flakes, for garnish

Dressing
1 cup oil
½ cup white wine vinegar
2 cloves garlic, crushed
2 cm fresh ginger root,
  peeled and grated
1 teaspoon ground cumin
salt and pepper

Combine cooked rice, capsicums, celery, shallots and water chestnuts. Combine dressing ingredients in a screwtop jar, shake, pour over salad and toss thoroughly. Cover and chill. Just before serving, toss again and garnish with toasted almond flakes.

Serves 8

Citrus Salad

1 lettuce, washed and dried
4 oranges, peeled and
  segmented
16 walnuts
1½ cups alfalfa
chopped fresh parsley, to
  garnish

Dressing
2 cloves garlic
juice 1 lemon
1 tablespoon white wine
  vinegar
pinch curry powder
salt
freshly ground black pepper
1 tablespoon olive or
  vegetable oil
1 teaspoon walnut oil

Toss lettuce in a bowl with orange segments, walnuts and alfalfa. Combine dressing ingredients in a screwtop jar and shake well. Pour over dressing before serving. Taste for seasoning and sprinkle with parsley.

Serves 4–6

Cucumber and Yoghurt Salad

Cauliflower and Broccoli Salad

500 g cauliflower
500 g broccoli
1 cup Creamy Vinaigrette
  Dressing (see recipe)
1–2 teaspoons French
  mustard
1 teaspoon capers, chopped
dash Tabasco sauce
paprika, to serve

Wash cauliflower and broccoli and separate into florets. Cook broccoli and cauliflower separately until tender but still crisp. Drain and cool. Combine dressing with mustard, capers and Tabasco sauce. Adjust seasonings to taste. Arrange cooked vegetables in a serving dish and spoon dressing over. Cover and chill until serving. Serve sprinkled with paprika.

Serves 10–12

Zucchini and Green Bean Salad

250 g zucchini, sliced 1 cm
  thick
250 g green beans, sliced
1 clove garlic, peeled
1 bay leaf
½ teaspoon salt
1 onion, sliced
1 red capsicum, sliced

Monticello Dressing
⅔ cup olive oil
sesame oil, to taste
⅓ cup tarragon or white
  wine vinegar
1 clove garlic, crushed
salt and pepper

Blanch zucchini and beans in small amount of water with garlic, bay leaf and salt for 5 minutes. Drain and refresh under cold water. Shake dry and combine with onion and capsicum. Shake dressing ingredients together in a screwtop jar, sprinkle over salad and toss. Serve immediately.

Serves 6

Tomato and Capsicum Salad

750 g tomatoes, peeled
1 bunch shallots, thinly
  sliced
3 green capsicums, sliced
⅓ cup Salad Dressing (see
  recipe)
⅓ cup Herbed Yoghurt
  Dressing (see recipe)

Cut tomatoes into wedges, discarding core section. Place in a bowl with shallots and capsicums. Mix dressings together and stir into salad. Serve chilled.

Serves 10–12

Salad Nicoise

Salade Nicoise

4 tomatoes, quartered
1 medium-sized onion,
  sliced thinly
1 green capsicum, seeded
  and sliced
1 red capsicum, seeded and
  sliced
12 radishes, thinly sliced
4 stalks celery, sliced
1 tablespoon finely
  chopped fresh basil
1 mignonette lettuce,
  washed and torn
185 g can tuna in oil
6 anchovy fillets, chopped
12 stuffed olives, halved
¼ cup Vinaigrette Dressing
  (see recipe)
1 tablespoon capers, to
  garnish
2 or 3 hard-boiled eggs,
  quartered, to garnish

Prepare vegetables and put into a large salad bowl. Fork through the tuna in oil, anchovies and olives.
  Pour Vinaigrette Dressing over and toss well. Decorate salad with capers and eggs. Serve chilled.

Serves 6

Top: Tomato and Capsicum Salad. Left: Cauliflower and Broccoli Salad

Barbecue Breads

Just about any bread goes with a barbecue. French bread sticks are hard to beat and so are wholewheat bread rolls, rye, black bread, plaits, herb breads and sour dough.

Few people have time to make bread these days, and why bother with so much excellent bread available from bread shops and delicatessens. There's nothing quite like plain old bread and butter, but for variety transform the standard loaf with herb or garlic butters (see recipes). For special barbecue occasions, try a traditional, pioneering-stock damper. It's easy to make, no kneading is necessary, it bakes in 25 minutes and makes a great impression.

Herbed Bread

1 Italian or Greek loaf
125 g butter
1 clove garlic, crushed
2 teaspoons finely chopped
    fresh parsley
1 teaspoon finely chopped
    fresh oregano
1 teaspoon finely chopped
    fresh dill
2 tablespoons grated
    Parmesan cheese

Cut bread diagonally into 2 cm slices without cutting through base. Combine butter, garlic and herbs and mix well. Spread on both sides of bread and sprinkle cheese over top. Lay on a piece of foil. Bring ends of foil up without closing in top to allow cheese to melt. Bake at 200°C (400°F) for 10 minutes.

Serves 6–8

Parsley Loaf

1 French or Vienna loaf
100 g butter
½ cup finely chopped fresh
    parsley
2 tablespoons grated cheese
1 teaspoon lemon juice

Slice bread 2 cm thick without cutting through base. Thoroughly mix remaining ingredients together and spread on both sides of bread. Wrap loaf in foil and heat through on the barbecue for 20–30 minutes.

Serves 6–8

Damper

3 cups self-raising flour
1 teaspoon salt
½ cup milk
½ cup water
80 g butter, softened

Sift flour and salt, mix in milk, water and butter until well combined. Form into round shape, slash top of dough to form a cross and place on tray. Bake in oven at 200°C (400°F) for 25 minutes. Damper sounds hollow when tapped.

Serves 4

Hot-filled Loaves

1 long French loaf

Cut bread diagonally into 2 cm slices without cutting through base. Spread with one of the following combinations.

Serves 6–8

French Onion Bread

250 g cream cheese
1 packet French onion soup
    mix

Combine ingredients and spread on both sides of the bread. Wrap loaf in foil and heat through on barbecue for 20–30 minutes.

Serves 6–8

Ham and Blue Cheese Bread

100 g butter
30 g blue vein cheese
1 tablespoon chopped fresh
    parsley
60 g ham, finely minced

Cream butter and cheese, add parsley and ham. Spread filling on both sides of bread, wrap bread in foil and heat on barbecue for 20–30 minutes.
Serves 6–8

Damper

Herbed Bread

Cheese and Chive Bread

60 g butter
250 g cream cheese
2 tablespoons chopped
  fresh parsley
2 tablespoons snipped fresh
  chives
2 tablespoons other
  chopped fresh herbs of
  your choice (optional)
freshly ground black pepper

Thoroughly mix butter and cream cheese. Add remaining ingredients and mix well. Spread mixture on both sides of bread. Wrap loaf in foil and heat through on the barbecue for 20–30 minutes.

Serves 6–8

Garlic and Herb Bread

3 cloves garlic, crushed
100 g butter
2 tablespoons chopped
  fresh parsley
pinch mixed dried herbs

Mix garlic with butter, then add parsley and herbs. Mix well. Spread filling on both sides of bread and wrap bread in foil. Heat on barbecue for 20–30 minutes.

Serves 6–8

Mussel Bread

105 g can smoked mussels,
  drained
250 g cream cheese
1 tablespoon chopped fresh
  parsley

Combine all ingredients and thoroughly mix. Spread on both sides of the loaf, wrap the loaf in foil and heat on barbecue for 20–30 minutes.

Serves 6–8

Left to right: Salad Dressing, Herbed Yoghurt Dressing, French Dressing, Tomato Dressing and Creamy Vinaigrette Dressing

Salad Dressing

2 tablespoons cornflour
⅔ cup low-fat milk
1 tablespoon prepared
  mustard
1 tablespoon margarine
1 egg, beaten
2 tablespoons vinegar
⅓ cup polyunsaturated oil
salt
freshly ground black pepper

Mix cornflour with a little milk. Heat remaining milk to simmering. Add cornflour mixture, stir well and simmer until thickened. Remove from heat and stir in mustard and margarine. Beat in egg, then gradually add vinegar and oil. Return mixture to pan and heat gently until thick, stirring constantly. Do not allow to boil. Allow dressing to cool. Add seasonings to taste. Use as directed.

Makes about 1¼ cups

Herbed Yoghurt Dressing

1 cup low-fat unflavoured
  yoghurt
2 tablespoons chopped
  fresh parsley
1 tablespoon snipped fresh
  chives
1 tablespoon prepared
  mustard
salt and freshly ground
  black pepper

Combine yoghurt, herbs and seasonings in a bowl. Store in an airtight container and refrigerate before using. Use as directed.

Makes about 1 cup

Vinaigrette Dressing

6 tablespoons oil,
  preferably olive oil
2 tablespoons white wine
  vinegar
1 clove garlic, crushed
  (optional)

½ teaspoon French mustard
pinch caster sugar
  (optional)
salt and freshly ground
  black pepper

Shake all ingredients in a jar until mixture thickens.

Makes about ¾ cup

Creamy Vinaigrette Dressing

This recipe is the basis of many fine salad dressings that add pizzazz to leafy green vegetables.

½ cup white wine vinegar
salt and freshly ground
  black pepper

1 cup olive oil or a
  combination of ½ olive
  oil and ½ vegetable oil

Combine all ingredients in a screwtop jar and shake.

Makes 1½ cups

French Dressing

¼ cup white wine vinegar
salt and freshly ground
  black pepper
½ teaspoon sugar

½ teaspoon mustard
  powder
1 clove garlic, peeled and
  lightly pressed
½ cup olive oil

Combine vinegar, salt and pepper, sugar, mustard and garlic in a screwtop jar or a blender. Shake or process until well blended. Gradually add oil and mix until combined.

Makes ¾ cup

Tomato Dressing

1 cup tomato juice
juice 1 lime or ½ lemon
2 shallots, finely chopped
2 cloves garlic, chopped

Worcestershire sauce
Tabasco sauce
freshly ground black pepper

Combine all ingredients and mix thoroughly. Store in an airtight container in the refrigerator. Use as directed.

Makes 1 cup

BARBECUE STARTERS

Delicious appetisers help you keep guests content while the main course is cooking. Not too many — you don't want to ruin appetites. Just a few tasty nibbles either prepared beforehand or cooked in a matter of minutes as the guests start arriving. Make sure you provide plenty of toothpicks and napkins to make the finger food easy to eat.

Angels on Horseback

12 fresh oysters
6 rindless bacon rashers

Cut bacon into 8 cm long strips and roll 1 around each oyster. Secure with a small skewer and barbecue taking care not to let the bacon burn. Serve hot with a seafood sauce. Barbecue time about 5–10 minutes.

Makes 12

Prawn Piggybacks

500 g uncooked prawns,
* shelled and deveined,*
* tails on*
125 g streaky bacon

Marinade
juice 2 lemons
equal quantity of olive oil
1 tablespoon dried tarragon
freshly ground black pepper
2 cloves garlic, crushed
* (optional)*

Combine marinade ingredients in a bowl and marinate prawns for at least 1 hour, turning occasionally. Thread 4 prawns on each skewer in pairs, turning the second one upside down and reversing direction. Cover with streaky bacon. Barbecue over a hot fire, taking care not to overcook. Prawns are ready when they turn pink. Just before serving, brush again with marinade. Barbecue time about 5–6 minutes.

Serves 6–8

Prawn Piggbacks served without the bacon (left) and Honeyed Prawns

Honeyed Prawns

1 kg cooked large prawns,
* shelled and deveined*

Marinade
1 cup dark honey
1 cup tomato sauce
½ cup salad oil
freshly ground black pepper
1 tablespoon dry mustard
dash Tabasco sauce

Combine marinade ingredients in a bowl and blend well. Marinate prawns 15–30 minutes then thread 2–3 prawns on each skewer and barbecue over a good hot fire. Brush with remaining marinade and turn. Barbecue time about 5–6 minutes.

Serves 6–8

Mini Clubs of Chicken

2 kg chicken wings

Marinade
½ cup soy sauce
2 cloves garlic, crushed
250 g Sate Sauce
½ cup water

Wash and dry wings. Cut off wing tips at joint (and save to make stock). Holding small end, pare around bone with sharp knife to cut meat free. Cut, scrape and push meat down over end of bone until wings look like little clubs. Combine marinade ingredients. Marinate wings overnight, drain, reserving marinade and baste while barbecuing over medium heat. Barbecue time about 10 minutes.

Serves 6–8

Mushroom and Caviar

medium-sized mushroom
* caps*
butter
pate
red and black caviar, for
* garnish*

Wipe mushroom caps clean. Place a small dob of butter in each cap and then fill with pate. Top with red or black caviar for garnish and just heat through on barbecue to warm. Barbecue time about 2 minutes.

Chicken Livers Indian

16 fresh chicken livers
2 bananas (almost ripe)
Madras curry powder
6 lean rindless bacon
  rashers

Cut livers in half or smaller if they are large. Slice banana into 1–2 cm thick slices sprinkling curry powder on both sides. Cut bacon into 3 cm lengths. Wrap together a piece each of liver and banana in bacon and serve with a small skewer. Barbecue gently until cooked, turning frequently. Barbecue time about 10–15 minutes.

Makes 24

Ham and Asparagus Rolls

8 slices leg ham, cut in half
16 green asparagus spears
cracked pepper

Place 1 asparagus spear on each half of leg ham. Roll up and serve with mini forks or toothpicks. Season with cracked pepper and serve.

Makes 16

Spiced Beef Meatballs

500 g extra lean mince
1 small onion, very finely
  chopped
2 eggs
fresh breadcrumbs
pinch garlic powder
Madras curry powder or
  Tandoori Mix
  (homemade or bought)

Mix mince, onion, eggs and breadcrumbs together so that meat will not fall apart. Add garlic and curry powder to taste and mix in thoroughly. Roll into 2.5 cm diameter meatballs, place on skewers and barbecue, taking care not to burn. Serve with a spicy sauce of your choice. Barbecue time about 10 minutes.

Makes 20, depending on size

Clockwise from top: Chicken Livers Indian, Spiced Meatballs, Ham and Asparagus Rolls, Mushroom and Caviar

Greek Appetiser Platter

Fruit Platter

½ pineapple, cut into
  pieces
1 ripe mango, cut into
  pieces
2 bananas, cut into pieces
  and sprinkled with lemon
  juice
1 coconut, broken into
  pieces (drain milk)
250 g fresh lychees
1 grapefruit, segmented
1 tablespoon sugar
fresh mint leaves, to garnish

Arrange fruit decoratively on a platter, and sprinkle lightly
with sugar. Garnish with mint leaves and serve chilled.

Serves 6

Serving suggestion: Line platter with banana leaves and
decorate with frangipani.

Greek Appetiser Platter

The Greek Appetiser Platter consists of an assortment of
light finger foods, served before a meal to whet the appe-
tite. The platter is filled with your choice of raw, cooked
and pickled vegetables, cheeses, fruits, bread, cold meats,
sausages and seafood.

150 g green olives
150 g black olives
1 teaspoon cracked
  coriander
1 clove garlic, crushed
1 tablespoon olive oil
2 tomatoes, quartered
1 soft-skinned cucumber,
  sliced thickly
200 g feta cheese, cut into
  2 cm cubes
200 g kasseri cheese, cut
  into 1 cm and 4 cm sticks
  (or other goat's milk
  cheese)
250 g cooked prawns,
  shelled
250 g pickled baby octopus
4 bread rolls, warmed and
  halved

Put olives into a bowl. Sprinkle with coriander, garlic and
olive oil. Mix and set aside.

  Arrange remaining ingredients, except the bread rolls,
on a large platter or prepare individual servings. Serve
with the warmed bread and the bowl of green and black
olives.

Serves 8

Create a beautiful fruit platter with a variety of exotic and tropical
fruits in season

BARBECUE ENTERTAINING

Barbecues make great parties. They are the easy way to feed large numbers of people with a minimum of fuss. With a little organisation much of the food can be prepared in advance, leaving everyone relaxed and free to mingle and enjoy the fun. Cooking is part of the fun.

What Kind of Party?

Barbecues are flexible. Bring a little imagination to choosing food and decorations and you can create completely different atmospheres. A buffet barbecue can be gourmet and glamorous or as casual as Sunday brunch with family and friends.

Children adore barbecues. Make their menu simple and fast. Foods like hamburgers, sausages and frankfurts are ideal. Hungry young mouths don't like to wait around too long! To keep them busy, ask them to make up their own kebabs choosing their meat, vegetables and fruits. They will have fun and the food will be nutritious.

Trust yourself

Creativity is the essence of barbecuing. It is as much a hobby as a cooking method — certainly it's an activity to be enjoyed in the preparation as much as in the eating. So taste as you go. I call it the 'TT' (Thumb Test). Check the sauces for seasonings. Add the flavour you favour. If you like garlic add it — if you hate it, leave it out. Trust your own taste buds and create!

A delicious Buffet Barbecue. Clockwise from top: Greek Salad, Barbecued Turkey Breast, Chicken Livers Indian and Fillet of Beef served with sauces, fresh fruit and bread

Choosing a Menu

Whatever the food, the main interest of the occasion usually centres on the barbecue itself. Part of the fun is watching the cook and the food, smelling the mouthwatering aromas and waiting — but not too long.

The secret of success is to be able to serve everyone hot food at the same time. To do this, shop carefully for your prawns or trout or same-sized chicken pieces; or cut food into same-sized portions before cooking. It is also important to be able to offer guests their steak cooked just the way they like it. If you have a fillet of beef, for example, you can offer rare, medium and well done steaks to your guests simply by carving from the thicker end (for rare) and the thinner (for well done).

Virtually every type of meat and seafood is suitable for barbecuing — pork, lamb, beef, chicken, fish, shellfish. Bastes add flavour during cooking, and sauces provide the right touch on the table. Make sure you label sauces — not everyone likes chilli. Don't forget vegetables and fruits. Vegetables should be cooked very briefly on the barbecue. Potatoes are terrific wrapped in foil and placed among the coals, but they can be cooked ahead of time and simply reheated on the barbecue. A good idea with onions is to blanch them briefly first in boiling water.

Complement the cooking with an array of interesting salads and breads prepared beforehand. If the cooking is going to take a while, hand around some simple appetisers to ward off hunger pangs. Choose titbits which you can prepare well ahead of time.

For dessert, offer flambe fruit or fruit kebabs from the barbecue or your favourite cold desserts prepared ahead of time.

Bamboo skewers

Remember to soak bamboo skewers well before using them. And don't cook with them too close to the fire, as they burn easily.

The Importance of Preparation

One of the most delightful things about a barbecue party is that it lets the host relax as much as the guests . . . that is, if the party has been well prepared.

Decide if you want to do all the cooking yourself or if you want to let guests — so long as there aren't too many — cook for themselves. Cooking is part of the fun. If you decide to let your guests help with the cooking, set up a raw food buffet next to the barbecue so everyone can help themselves. Salads, breads and accompaniments should be at a separate table to avoid congestion near the cooking area.

Barbecue plans should include the possibility of bad weather. Rain doesn't have to spoil a barbecue. Either cook the food outside on a portable barbecue in a sheltered spot or move everything indoors and use your oven.

Make a checklist of everything you require, from food, to crockery and decorations. Make sure you have lots of plates (not just one per person) and utensils, as people tend to put them down and forget them.

Prepare those dishes which can be made ahead — such as desserts, starters and salads — long before the guests arrive, the day before if possible. You'll then be calm and relaxed when the door bell rings.

Set up the buffet tables well in advance too and provide plenty of seats. Barbecues are generally informal occasions but most people still find it very difficult to eat, drink and hold a handbag standing up. Use cushions and rugs if you don't have enough chairs.

It is a good idea to collect everything to be taken out to the barbecue on a food trolley. You'll save time and energy that way.

Plan the order in which you'll cook the food so that there's a constant supply of beautiful hot food. Some foods like sausages can be kept warm at the side of the grill, others, like fillet of steak, must be served the minute they are cooked.

Stuffed Sausages, Chipolatas, Frankfurts, Burgers 'n' Buns and Hamburgers served with salad and sauce will be a big favourite for a Children's Barbecue

Guests, family members, neighbours, friends, business associates — everyone feels more relaxed out of doors. And that's why more Australians are holding cocktail and birthday parties, neighbourhood gatherings, weddings and other functions right in their own backyard.

Casual, outdoor entertaining has reached such acceptance, even in the evenings, that there are few homes that don't own some sort of barbecue either constructed in the garden or tucked away on wheels in the shed or garage.

What started out as a simple grill over a metal pan has now reached great heights of sophistication in design and performance. Thousands of portable units are sold each year while almost as many people decide to take up tools and build their own.

The Total Landscape

So, before you decide where to site your barbecue, it's a good idea to look at your available space and plan a total entertainment area. Too often, barbecues are located in an obscure corner of the garden; a location rarely ideal for entertaining or relaxing. Ideally, the barbecue should be integrated into the overall look of your house and garden.

The way you landscape your garden and position the various facilities may make all the difference to your success as a host or hostess. With a little forethought and planning you can create a comfortable, functional area where guests will enjoy themselves as opposed to a cramped, draughty spot where a meal becomes a hazard.

There are many variables to consider: positioning must allow for the sun and the wind, what to do about smoke, fumes, smells, buzzing insects and burnt sausages. There's also the question of where to place outdoor furniture. So, before you get started on installing your dream barbecue, planning a total entertainment environment is essential.

First, consider the number of people you're likely to have at any one gathering. It would be very uncomfortable to cram say 30 people into a corner between the pool and the patio. The cook and the guests should have ample room to move around without jostling each other.

Choosing a Site

The best site in any garden is a level area so your first step in preparing to construct a barbecue and landscape the garden may be to level a given area. You will also need easy access to the kitchen such as a paved walkway, without steps if possible.

Before anything is built into your garden, check with your local council; you may need permission to build in some areas. The next step is to finalise the actual siting of your barbecue. If you have a pool, or hope to build one later on, it's a good idea to have the barbecue reasonably handy to it. Pool parties and barbecued food go hand in hand.

Because you have to carry food and utensils from the kitchen to the barbecue, it may be necessary to locate it near the house. However, the disadvantage with this arrangement is that smoke and barbecue smells may linger in the home.

Consider the Neighbours

Wherever you site your barbecue, make sure that it will not inconvenience or annoy your neighbours. A barbecue sited in a corner of the garden may look attractive but it could mean black smoke descending onto your next door neighbour's washing line.

If smoke is a problem, you may need to construct a chimney which will also make things more comfortable for the chef. Here again, you will have to consult with your local council.

If you decide to site your barbecue a long way from the kitchen, it's a good idea if all tools, utensils and crockery are stored in a hamper and carried to the site in one load. Alternatively, a good trolley may be the answer.

The Importance of Lighting

Lighting is extremely important for everyone's comfort. It also means convenience for the barbecue chef and it can add just the right atmosphere to any festive gathering. Permanent lighting should be planned right from the very beginning as underground cables may have to be laid.

Planning should also include the options of diffused or sharp light, conspicuous flood lighting or skilfully camouflaged illuminations as part of the overall 'look' of the garden. Another option is temporary lighting which usually involves hurricane lamps or decorative lanterns. Low voltage bulbs give a softer effect and durable fittings must be installed to cope with all types of weather.

Consider too how your chosen light fittings will look in the day time and always locate switches in accessible, convenient spots. Remember too that lights attract mosquitoes so guests will appreciate some insect repellent coils, candles or wands. Naturally, all lighting fixtures must be installed by a qualified electrician.

Barbecues to Suit the Scenery

Ideally, the style of barbecue you choose should blend aesthetically with the surroundings and the purpose for which you intend it. You can either build the entire barbecue yourself or buy a kit variety. It's also possible to buy a ready-made barbecue which is just waiting to be slotted into the chosen site.

Take into consideration the environment, the materials from which your home is built, your garden and other aspects before choosing bricks or other construction materials. For example, a bright brick barbecue, placed next to a sandstone cottage would be an eyesore.

You should also take into account the style of your garden. A large garden with lots of trees and lush greenery would be able to take a big, high barbecue more readily than a smaller garden with low flower beds. If your garden is surrounded by bushland, it may be best to design a barbecue with a lid which ensures that no stray sparks cause fires.

Don't plan an enormous barbecue with multiple grills and lots of storage which takes up wanted space, if you plan to have a barbecue for the family twice a year. Whatever design you decide upon, your barbecue should be functional, sited carefully and add to the overall decorative look of your outdoor entertaining area.

Index